Morning Star of the Reformation

by Andy Thomson

Bob Jones University Press, Greenville, South Carolina 29614

Morning Star of the Reformation

Edited by Mark Sidwell

Cover and illustrations by Stephanie True

©1988 Bob Jones University Press
Greenville, South Carolina 29614

ISBN 0-89084-453-4

Printed in the United States of America

20   19   18   17   16   15   14   13   12

My warmest thanks to Edward Panosian, Ph.D., Ron Horton, Ph.D., and Miss Judy Groff, M.A.

Dedicated to
Mrs. Marie Bayer

Contents

Publisher's Note

The scene is medieval Oxford in England: a historic city; a crossroads of culture; a city with close ties to royalty and to the political upheavals of the whole burgeoning country. Oxford's university was the center of intense intellectual activity, and it dominated the philosophical thought of medieval England.

To this many-storied place with its gray stone halls came John of Wycliffe—a wide-eyed youth from Yorkshire in the north of England. He came to be a student at the university, and he stayed, despite the rigors of university life and the horrors of the Pestilence. He became one of the outstanding intellectual figures of the fourteenth century.

Wycliffe's dispute with the Roman Catholic Church over abuses of the clergy, transubstantiation, and papal supremacy soon marked him as a heretical reformer. His views, however, coincided with the increasingly clamorous demands for reform in church and state by many learned Englishmen. Although the Duke of Lancaster, John of Gaunt, supported Wycliffe for his own political purposes, his protection delayed the inevitable persecution and allowed Wycliffe's influence to spread beyond England to Europe.

Wycliffe's most enduring legacy, however, is the English translation of the Bible, which he instigated and his followers completed. It became the best English version of the Scriptures until the time of Tyndale, more than a century later.

His disciples, called Lollards, took the English Bible to the people of the countryside, urging those who could to read it for themselves and to find salvation in Christ alone instead of in the "Mother Church." Despite terrible persecution, the Word was spread abroad, opening the hearts of the common folk and preparing the way for the great upheaval of the coming Reformation.

We have the same Word today, in translations more accurate and abundant than any person in the fourteenth century could have dreamed of. May the reader be challenged by this story of an intrepid and brilliant man: challenged to treasure the Word and to feed upon it for himself.

"They that be wise shall shine as the brightness of the firmament; and they that turn many to righteousness as the stars for ever and ever." (Daniel 12:3)

PART ONE

Chapter One
Two Travelers
Autumn, 1345

My name is William Ayleton, and you, if you saw me, would think me a doddering old man on his way to the grave. The priests and abbots who pass me by think me a poor beggar. They think age has mixed my brains. I let them think it.

To you, I would unfold my story, and I would share with you the contents of a little book that I hide in my clothes.

Well you may ask what the book is. If I were caught with it, I should be burned alive. The pope would condemn me. The king would condemn me. I would be called a devil, and the peasant boys would run circles around me to catch a glimpse of my horns and tail. The women would fear me, making the sign of the cross to protect themselves. And some would think me guilty of witchcraft, all because of this book that I carry.

But surely you are educated. You know better. What is the little book that they fear? What is the book that would condemn me to death in England? The Bible, of course.

Perhaps you have heard that the English are free. Yes, we proudly boast that we are. More free, certainly, than the poor French, who are driven and hounded by noblemen and clergymen alike. And more free than the poor souls of Italy, who have been slaughtered and left dead by the hundreds in the cold Alpine mountains while one rival pope poured out his wrath against the peasants of another.

But I get ahead of myself. My story begins almost ninety years ago. In fact, my story begins before I was even born, when a bold and dashing archer first struck up a friendship with a young scholar on the road from Leicester.

It was the autumn of 1345. A cold dusk shadowed the Leicester Road. There would be no stars to brighten the sky this night, for swollen clouds hung overhead. Already they were threatening to drop their chill rain on any wayfarers caught outside.

A young man, scarce fourteen years old, squinted at the roadside as he hurried along, seeking shelter.

"Hallo!" someone called. "Hallo ahead!"

He stopped and waited. It might be a farmer who would offer him a bed for the night in exchange for chores. He hoped so.

That was why the newcomer, a strapping lad of seventeen or so, saw the disappointment in the younger traveler's face. The big lad's name was Sebastian Ayleton, and he sported not only a new tunic with flaring sleeves but also new stockings and a wide belt. He was *not* a farmer. In fact, he carried a stout yew stave, which—at second glance—turned out to be a longbow.

"What ails you?" he asked. "There's a sour face for my cheery hello."

The younger boy suddenly laughed. "Pardon me, I beg you. I had hoped you were a farmer with a dry roof to offer me for the night."

"Nay, a fellow traveler like yourself. But there's an inn a mile ahead. What's your name, lad?"

"John of Wycliffe, and you?"

"Sebastian Ayleton." And he slapped himself on his massive chest.

It is his story that I record here, for Sebastian Ayleton was the man who became my father, and he it was who made fast friends with John Wycliffe. Neither knew on that day that they would soon see the world turned upside down, nor that the very road on which they stood would soon be made a waste place by God's wrath. They only knew that they were hungry and weary on the road at dusk.

"Ah, I think you'll be alone at the inn, good Sebastian," John said. "I cannot spare for it. I've yet to purchase books and school vestures."

Sebastian Ayleton waved away the objection. "I cannot afford a bed, either. But fear not, I'll get us in, my Master Johannes."

"You are bound for Oxford?"

"Aye. I saw you far ahead and have hurried on to catch you. You keep a swift pace for one so slight. From the wild country, are you?" he added with a glance at the rustic wool tunic and patched stockings that John wore.

"Aye. York. Near Richmond."

"And I from Leicester. My father is away on the continent, fighting." And Sebastian Ayleton's sparkling brown eyes blazed as at a sudden longing. Then he gave a snort of disgust. "And I go to Oxford to pray for his soul."

In those days, of course, nearly all the students at Oxford became priests by taking the sacrament of holy orders. And many a student was sent to Oxford to pray for the souls of his family. The *Paternoster,* or "Our Father," was the most common prayer—that and the *Ave,* or "Hail Mary."

Sebastian patted the unstrung bow, which stood as high as his head. "I can fire off an arrow and shoot two more before it comes to earth, friend John, yet now I am doomed to kneel at mass all morning and quote the scholars from noon to sunset."

"Perhaps your father will relent before you take holy orders," John suggested.

"More likely he'll be split from head to belt in some skirmish, and I shall be freed," Sebastian grumbled.

"Sebastian! And about your own father!"

"Pardon, pardon. I think you're already the priest of this parish from the way you talk so, Father John."

"Holy orders is a serious thing. You enter it with too loose and light a tongue."

Sebastian gave a snort and said, "My milk and meat have been the tales of hot skirmishes, final charges, and bold, crafty shots loosed from an archer's bow. And then—after a close skirmish with the French—my father decides to put me where I'll keep his soul safe: with a bunch of ox-eyed, soft-handed, big-bellied *priests!*" He glanced sharply at John. "Do you truly think them a bunch of holy men?"

"I had supposed so," John told him.

"Are not there Cistercian monasteries near Richmond in York?" Sebastian asked. "What think you of them?"

"I'd never thought of them before," John admitted. "Except that when the Scots would raid us, we often fled to one of the walled monasteries."

"Then I'll tell you," Sebastian said. "The monasteries are not the holy places that they claim to be. Instead, they are little kingdoms. The monks own vast tracts of land, and they have peasant farmers who work for them. They keep their farmers under a double load of taxation and then charge rent from them. And a farmer cannot grind his own grain. Nay, he must take it to the abbey, and they will grind it and charge him. And if he's caught with a small grinder in his own home, he's shorn of his ears or has a hand lopped off. And a sheep keeper cannot full his own cloth. Nay, he must take it to the monastery, where they will full it and take their portion and then overcharge him. Now tell me, is this the service where you will lay up treasure in heaven?"

John hesitated. He was, as Sebastian had noted, a rustic country lad. Little had he ever seen of monastic life, though he had seen the lands under the domain of the Cistercian monastery in Richmond—huge tracts of land: farm, meadow, and wood. John's father had been adamant that John should not be a monk but rather a parish priest. Was that why?

he wondered. Perhaps his father also resented the fact that the monks lived rich and at ease while poor men starved. Of course, it would never have been safe for John's father to have condemned the monks. John's father was far from wealthy, but as lord of Wycliffe manor, he would be held accountable for his words. Sebastian, on the other hand, had the freedom to say what he thought, and he made the most of that freedom.

"Such for the monks," Sebastian said. "Then there are those rascals the friars, who go begging about the countryside, sticking their noses in where they're not—"

"Hush, friend Sebastian," John said gently. "You have given me enough to think on for one night. My mind is reeling from these thoughts. In truth, I've been too rustic and backward."

Something in Sebastian's manner changed at the frank confession. "Well, John," he said in a softer tone. "It's a wide world, but I had not meant to deter you from your vocation. You'll make a good priest, I don't doubt, though perhaps the first in all England. But stay." He put a hand on John's shoulder. "Here's the Dark Ferret. You wait outside here, and I will make arrangements."

John took a step after him as Sebastian made for a long, low house with a thatched roof. "But—"

"Nay, do as I bid in this," Sebastian said. "I will get them used to one of me before I let them know we are two. It is good diplomacy. Stay until I bid you enter."

"As you say, then. But the rain is nearer as well as the dark."

"I will hurry."

And, stringing his bow before he went in, Sebastian strode to the door and vanished inside the inn, leaving John Wycliffe on the road.

Chapter Two
At the Inn of the Dark Ferret

John stood in the road in the gathering dark, measuring his time with the *Aves* and *Paternosters* that he mumbled under his breath. It had never occurred to him that the ceaseless rambling of Latin prayers in order to measure time might be a sacrilegious practice. In a land of few clocks, every farmhand, squire, clerk, and bishop counted out the passing minutes by repetitions of prayers.

After thirty *Paternosters* and half as many *Aves,* Sebastian Ayleton returned to the door of the Dark Ferret and beckoned John to enter. And not a moment too soon. The door scarce closed again behind John when the rain came down with a *woosh.* It was a cold autumn rain, common enough in October. Young John of Wycliffe must have felt a throb of gratitude to his new friend for finding a place for him at the inn, out of the weather and out of the dark.

The interior of the Dark Ferret was dim, with a clutter of chairs and men and a long table made by laying smooth boards across trestles. There was a hearth along one wall, with a huge and bubbling pot over the fire. John's insides knotted hungrily at the thought of supper.

As John later told me when I came to know him, he had left home eight days before with plenty of bread and some cheese in his scrip, along with ten silver coins wrapped up in a piece of cloth.

Yet the bread and cheese were long gone, and the young man was at pains not to touch the silver coins. For when he arrived at Oxford, the money must be intact to purchase his school robes, books, and any other items necessary to a new clerk. His tuition was taken care of, for he had qualified for a special scholarship granted to six students from the wild northern counties. His father had paid the balance. Otherwise, John was on his own.

His eyes slowly grew accustomed to the dim room. There were a few men—farmers, to judge by their tunics—bunched in one corner, talking together and drinking from the leather cups commonly used at inns.

In another corner, a tall lank man with scraggly white hair that hung askew from under a red cap reclined in one chair with his feet propped up on another. The road dust lay heavy on his leather shoes and was spattered up his legs. It was plain that he was a traveler—probably a merchant— able to prop up and sleep anywhere when the day was done. He slept with his mouth hung open, and his snores all but drowned out the drumming of the rain.

There were no other chairs available; so the two young men sat on the benches at the table.

"Why do the three in the corner look on you so darkly?" John asked.

"Oh, it is nothing, John, nothing," Sebastian said airily. He ran his thick fingers through his curly brown hair. "Many a man holds a grudge unworthily 'gainst another. Look not on them, and they shall forget us anon."

My father could pretend great ignorance and carelessness when he wanted to, and so John obediently turned from gazing at the three yeoman farmers and soon had other things to think of. The dame of the house appeared from the kitchen, carrying on a tray the huge slabs of bread called *trenchers* by the practical English tongue.

The three yeomen came up to the table, and even the sleeper woke up to take his seat. When each had his trencher of bread before him, the woman brought the stew from the fire and ladled it with an iron spoon onto the bread.

A younger girl came out with a platter of leather cups for the newcomers and spoons for all. John forgot everything else as he ate. The others were also busy with their food.

"By my ten skilled fingers!" Sebastian exclaimed. "A knight of the realm could fare no better than this, eh, John?"

"I think not, yet hunger is always the best sauce," John added. He looked rueful. "And I am always hungry."

"You? *Mon enfant*," Sebastian exclaimed in poor French, *"tu es maigre comme un clou!"* (You are as thin as a nail!)

French was a language still spoken commonly in England, often interspersed freely with English dialects. John guessed that Sebastian had grown up hearing it from his father and the other archers who had spent time in France. "You hardly seem the glutton, little Father John," Sebastian added.

"It seems to vanish on me, in truth," John agreed. "And I might as well not waste the time and victuals that I do in eating, for I get no bigger. It would be better to keep my flesh down and refrain, I suppose."

"Time later to keep the flesh down," Sebastian said, draining his cup at one draught. He waved it for more.

"Nay, it's a sin to be a glutton," John retorted.

"You, a glutton? Mayhap a scarecrow could be a glutton. No, *mon fils,* take no offence, but one so pinched to the bones ought to fear other sins than gluttony. Eat up! Eat up! And may your patron make you stout! You should have been named Sebastian!" And he thumped himself on the chest. "Aye, St. Sebastian, the patron of archers, he's a sturdy one. Now, you take John the Baptist—no solid food but locusts. Aye, no wonder you're slight. He never set any store by victuals."

"But he turned all Israel upside down," John ventured. "And he was the one chosen to prepare the way for the Saviour."

"Ah! Well, may you turn all England upside down, St. John of Wycliffe!"

"Sebastian, hush," John said. "You speak perilous close to sacrilege."

"Oh, have no fear of that! None of our bold comrades here are monks, eh, comrades?"

The merchant took no heed of the comment, but the three yeomen glowered at Sebastian as though there was ill feeling between him and them. He laughed at them. "Shall we have another go, *messieurs?*" he asked.

John glanced at him. The farmers paid their debt for the meal and silently left the inn.

"Your ill-mannered jokes have chased away the dame's business!" John exclaimed. "What did you do that made them angry?"

Sebastian turned his attention to the rest of his food and said, "Nothing, John, nothing. 'Twas an honest contest between honest men, but I won."

John was silent while Sebastian ate, but at last the younger man began to understand. "Sebastian," he asked, "did you gamble with them?"

"Aye, I offered four pence to the man who could draw my bowstring back to the ear. I demonstrated how easy it was, but each one tried and failed in turn, and thus I won the price of our night's lodging."

John stood up but Sebastian pulled him down. "It's paid and done, Father John. The woman of the house expects us, and those farmers are long gone."

"Sebastian, you'll ever be a heart scald to the Church," John predicted. "You accuse so many of so much, yet are guilty of the same yourself."

"I've not taken orders yet, John," he returned. "It's my hope to escape this somehow."

Chapter Three
A Sorry Sight

Sebastian Ayleton slept easily that night on the bed he had gambled for. But John of Wycliffe did not sleep as well. For it had already begun to dawn on him that the Church—that which he had always called the Holy Mother Church—was rotten on the inside. He was but a boy yet, and he had no answers, nor even a bit of Scripture to comfort him.

A cool autumn morning dawned on October the eighth. John of Wycliffe and Sebastian Ayleton were on the road just after first light, having taken a piece of toasted bread apiece from the dame of the house. In return they promised to give a prayer for her soul at every shrine they came to along the way to Oxford.

Sebastian was much less talkative that morning, and John was still pondering yesterday's discussions; so they walked for some miles in silence.

Coming around a steep part in the road, they could look down on a scattering of thatch-roofed huts and some sparse fields. The morning air was still fresh and clean and somehow bracing. But it was just as they cleared the curve in the road that both travelers saw a gruesome sight dangling from a long tree limb which jutted out over the roadway. It was a hanged man. The wind drove his body around a bit, first in a little circle one way, then in a little circle back again.

"Preserve us!" John cried, and Sebastian started back and took his yew bow in his hand as though minded to string it at need. You may laugh at them for being cowards, when hangings are as common as fleas these days, but it is one thing to witness an execution at midday among the crowd and quite another to stumble upon a hanged man in the lonely woods in the gray dawn light.

John recovered first. "Nay," he said, and some color returned to his cheeks. "He can do us no harm now, Sebastian. Alas, poor soul. Rather we should pity him than draw back. Come, we must pass by."

Side by side they approached the hanged man, whose heels, dangling, were at about their own head level.

"He's not been long dead," John said.

"There's a paper pinned to his belt," Sebastian said.

"Perhaps the charges laid against him," John guessed. "Let us leave him in peace and go on."

"He needs no charges written 'gainst him," Sebastian said, growing braver and drawing nearer to the corpse. "Look you, and you might easily discern his trade: the long knife sheath, empty, the second sheath shoved in his belt, the dark hood to cover his face, and the many pockets torn out. He was a robber and a violent man, I take it. See the scar from nose to ear. An old scar, think ye?"

John came a little nearer, and his eyes were softened by pity. "Aye. A robber and cutthroat. We ought to pray for his soul, but in truth, there's little hope for him now."

"You may say so, but see the paper!" Sebastian said, then clumsily read out a few Latin words, stopped, and shrugged. "The script is too bad for my uncouth eyes, yet I perceive that a pardoner got to him before he died."

As you may well know, the Church's pardoners are those men who have her blessing to go out and sell "indulgences" for certain sins. The reasoning was that enough good deeds had been laid up in heaven for the Church to become their broker to worthy people. The only way to measure whether people were worthy was to see how much money they would part with in order to buy up saintly merits.

The pardoners in that day were very free to sell forgiveness to criminals. In fact, some pardoners would accompany the sheriffs on the chase, just to be present when a criminal was caught and hanged. The pardoner would worm as much money from the doomed man as possible before giving him the paper from Mother Church that proclaimed him forgiven by God. It was commonly done in the days of my father's youth, and so the sight of the "plenary indulgence," or pardon, did not surprise Sebastian at all. But John was shocked, for he had been trained up to believe that only very holy and mournful people would be granted an indulgence by the Church.

John stepped closer. "It is as you say! This is an indulgence to heaven itself! Surely it's a forgery!"

Sebastian glanced at him. "Why say you so? Surely a robber would have the money to buy into paradise. All it takes is a contrite heart and fifteen pieces of gold."

"Nay, it cannot be! Who would dare claim that a careless robber may enter heaven for fifteen bits of gold?" John cried.

"The blood of the Saviour and the merits of the saints lie in store," Sebastian said. "Why do you shake? Do you fear his ghost?"

"Nay!" John exclaimed. But he trembled from head to foot. "Let us go, Sebastian! Pray, let us go!" And he turned away and hurried on.

Sebastian followed. "Stay John, not so fast," the big archer said, catching up. "What ails you?"

"Alas, what a country rustic I have been!" John cried. "I have walked the length of England these last eight days and one and seen all the wickedness I thought one man could bear. Yet now—since but last night—I have seen twice as much, and done by our own Church, where you and I go to take holy orders."

"I have shattered your innocence," Sebastian said soberly. "Spoken overmuch and rudely thrust all manner of ills into your conscience. Forgive me, John."

"Nay, Sebastian, I should have seen it all presently. Take no blame to yourself. But woe unto us. God the righteous Judge shall come, and what shall we say to Him? That we offered grace for money? That we have proclaimed ourselves followers of Christ as a means to gain learning and stature? And what of the abbeys and abbots that you spoke of? The monks and the monasteries? How shall they compare themselves to the poverty that Christ and his disciples suffered?"

How right and how true his words were, and how well did he predict the wrath of God. Sebastian Ayleton never did forget those words of his friend, for not many months from then they did see the wrath of God fall. The abbeys and abbots were struck down; the vast fields of the monasteries were left to rot. Men were shortly to die by the thousands every day.

But on that morning Sebastian tried to shrug off John's fears. He affected his carefree humor and said, "You speak an argument many years old: that Christ was poor and the abbots rich. But come, cheer up, John. We've heard only half the story. At Oxford perhaps they will teach us how to mend all."

Chapter Four
Oxford

"Aye, this smells like scholarship," Sebastian quipped as they came into sight of the many spires, towers, and tiled roofs of the bustling town.

The city of Oxford and its university sat flush against a marshland on one side and a river on the other. As the two young men walked down to the gates, the many smells of a town greeted them: the blood of slaughtered animals, manure, the faint and pleasant smoke of many a hearth, and the reek of burning trash.

Both were silent as they entered the town, for they felt a little shy. The streets in the town were perilously dark and narrow. Sebastian instinctively led the way through the mill of people and horse carts that clattered together over the cobbles.

Precious little sunlight managed to get through the high barricade of two-story buildings that seemed all pushed together. The predominant color was gray: grayed old timbers that framed the sturdy private houses, taverns, shops, halls, and churches. The plaster that had been used to fill the timber frames was also gray. So much road dust had been kicked up against the walls by the passing crowds that all of the other color was lost. And the tile roofs were gray—somewhat pale from exposure to sun and wind.

At times Sebastian pushed and shoved and argued to get them through the milling people. Tomorrow was St. Denis Day, the opening of the autumn term, and the whole town was astir while the students gathered in to the university.

The men of Oxford passed by with many a squint, especially at John's coarse woolen tunic. He indeed looked like a poor farm boy compared to them in their tunics with the flared shoulders, wide sleeves, and tapered waists.

At long last Sebastian found the town square. He turned to John. "Where now?"

"I have a cousin who lives in Balliol Hall," John told him. "He's secured a place for me there and a scholarship. What about you, Sebastian?"

"Balliol Hall's good enough for me," Sebastian said. "One'll be as dank and wormy as another, I'll warrant."

"Let us ask directions, then," John suggested. He held out a hand to a passerby. "Friend—"

The man knocked John's arm away. "Hands off, you filth!" he cried and rushed by.

Sebastian tried and was also repulsed as "a college hall cockroach."

"Patience, Sebastian," John advised. "Your patron meekly suffered many arrows. Let us be like him and forbear." He turned to a passing friar, hoping for better luck. "I pray thee, good—" But the friar went on without a glance. Just then there was a *crack* of wood on bone. John spun 'round to see Sebastian, his stout wood bow in one hand, and a Dominican friar caught by the collar in the other hand.

"Pray, not so fast, friend," Sebastian growled, holding the bow up as though he would crack the man over the head a second time.

The poor man, who had a red welt coming up on his head, collected his dazed wits and then sputtered, "Disease take you, loutish oaf! Take your carnal hands off me—"

"Speak so hot and I'll crack you again!" Sebastian bellowed, shaking the poor man.

"Nay, pardon, 'twas but the flesh that spoke. How may I help you?" the man said quickly.

"What is the way to Balliol Hall? And speak truth or I shall come a-searching for you with an arrow on the string."

"Down Horsemonger Street, all the way past the stables and horse markets. You'll know it by the new chapel with the large glass window."

Sebastian let him go with a surly, "We thank you."

The friar kicked him in the shin and raced away.

John caught the big archer's arm. "Stay, Sebastian, have pity. What would he think, the way you cracked his pate?"

"He was but a Dominican. There was nothing inside."

My father, like many a free Englishman, despised the Dominican friars. They were—even back then—in charge of keeping the Church "pure," and in that day they had already brought their torture chambers to every country but England. Oh, happy days now gone, when we were free of them! Edward, our good king, would not permit the Dominicans to torture or burn heretics. The Dominicans therefore chafed to get the Englishmen, and the Englishmen chafed to drive out the Dominicans.

"Your ways are direct, I grant you," John told him. "Perhaps next time you will not be so rough."

"Rough? *Ma foi!* You haven't seen *rough* yet, John."

"Perhaps not," John agreed. "But come, let us find these horse stables and the hall. My cousin William will be awaiting us."

They found the hall according to the friar's directions, and there they found John's cousin William, a well groomed, fashionable young man who seemed to be much better off than John, to Sebastian's eyes.

Introductions were made, and William told them, "Board is fifteen pence a week here, though Johannes, you'll pay only three a week. Come. If you're agreeable, you must sign the roll."

He led them from the street inside the hall, where it was dim. As their eyes adjusted, John and Sebastian got a look at the refectory, where their meals would be served, and they noticed that everywhere else, crude, thin partitions had carved up the hall into tiny cubicles. Students slept four to a cubicle and used the center of the hallways for a study. On the hallway where they were to live, stools had been set up outside the cubicles, for those who wished to sit. Light streamed in through unglazed windows in this part of the building.

Both boys were duly introduced to the Master of the hall, Hugh of Corbrigge, and they signed the roll, thus officially becoming students of Oxford University.

"It is the saddest day of my life," Sebastian said gloomily. Little did he know what he would live to see.

Chapter Five
The Initiates

That day and the next passed in a whirl of running to buy books, and clothes, and a shave.

On the evening of St. Denis Day, John, Sebastian, and the other new clerks at Oxford filed in a straggling procession into St. Mary's Church. The beard and head of each young man had been newly shaved, or tonsured, and each one wore the brightly colored tunic, the sleeveless robe, and the fur hood that marked him as an Oxford man. The men of the hall where John and Sebastian lived had chosen red for their color that year, and so the two initiates and their fellows from Balliol wore red tunics under their sleeveless cappas. Men from other halls wore yellow or blue or green.

They heard mass and then came to the altar to be received into the Church as subdeacons. After mass. there were still other details to be attended to: voting on the rules of conduct in the hall, deciding how chores should be appointed and how discipline was to be administered.

The hall was dark by the time all was said and done. John and Sebastian groped their way to their cubicle, which they shared with two others, undressed, and found the straw pallets that were their beds.

Sebastian let out a groan of weary pleasure as he stretched out his long limbs.

The two other men stumbled in and quickly found the other two pallets. They were also new and had both become subdeacons that day.

"Don't forget, mass tomorrow," one said in a low voice.

"Be that you, Fleet Nigel?" Sebastian asked.

"Aye."

"I heard some of the fellows saying your name down in the hall," he added. "How did you ever come by such a title?"

"I ran messages as a boy, only I was the slowest and stoutest of the lot, so they called me Fleet Nigel."

Sebastian burst out with a guffaw which he barely smothered, and somebody from the next cubicle banged on the wall for silence.

"Who is the other?" Sebastian whispered.

"Giles," the fourth whispered back.

"We are Sebastian and John. When is mass?"

"Late in the morning," Fleet Nigel whispered. "We'll not break fast until after noontime."

"We fasted today and we'll fast tomorrow," Sebastian growled. "A body could die before the term begins."

"Quiet!" someone bellowed. "Whatever rogue speaks from here to dawn shall be thrashed!"

"Aye!" several shouted in chorus.

Sebastian, grumbling, settled back in silence. One by one the four new students dropped off to sleep.

But at mass the next morning, Sebastian found many things to occupy his mind and take his thoughts off food. Unlike the straggling, unpracticed procession of the new clerks the day before, the procession of the Doctors, Masters, Bachelors, and undergraduates was very imposing and colorful indeed. He also noticed that the students from the monasteries and those of the friars sat together on the opposite side of the church from those training to become parish priests.

Sebastian knew that the monasteries such as the Cistercians and Benedictines sent their bright young men to school. And the friars, such as the Dominicans and Franciscans, also sent theirs to school. The young monks and friars at Oxford were cared for by their orders. But John and Sebastian, since they didn't belong to one of the orders of monks or friars, paid their own way. They were training to become parish priests, and since they would someday be saying mass and conducting the sacraments for the secular people, they were called *seculars*.

The whole time the mass progressed, Sebastian watched the men from the orders across the aisle, and his fingers itched for his stout yew bow. The monks and the friars were looking at the seculars with no great love. He wondered why. After all, the monks and friars were the ones who paid no tuition and no board. Their orders saw them through the university. And while the poor seculars slept on straw and ate black bread, those from the orders slept on mattresses and had roast mutton.

The more Sebastian thought of it, the less he liked them and the less welcome did he find their sneers of contempt and disdain. He loudly cracked his knuckles. John poked him in the ribs.

"Why do those dogs glare at us so?" Sebastian asked in a low voice.

"Peace, Sebastian. This is mass," John whispered.

On his other side, Fleet Nigel whispered back, "They hate us because the seculars control the university by order of the King, and God bless him!"

"Amen to that, but—" Sebastian cut himself off as Hugh of Corbrigge turned around farther up and glared back at them.

After mass was ended and the long and colorful procession had filed out, the men of each hall went to get their breakfast at the hall refectory.

Balliol's refectory was large and plain, with a single long table set on trestles. They sat down at the table, and each man received a round loaf of bread.

"It takes more than this for a man of my frame," Sebastian said in disgust.

"Giles and I found a handy place with herring to offer, smoking hot," Fleet Nigel said. "Perhaps a visit there after our penance here—"

"Ho! That's for me!" Sebastian agreed. "What say you, John?"

John must have felt nearly as hungry as his big friend, but already his little collection of silver coins had dwindled. "Nay, I—"

"Oh come! I'll get us in!"

John became firm. "Nay, Sebastian, I—"

Sebastian waved away the objection. "I have money, friend John. No tricks, I promise. You'll be my guest."

"A handsome invitation!" Fleet Nigel exclaimed. "Come on then, John. Your eyes are hungry enough."

"Aye, and dull books will be our lot before long," Giles added. "Let us eat our fill and be merry 'round the table while we may."

"Well, I will then, and many thanks," John agreed.

"There's our trencherman," Sebastian said with a laugh. "We'll make him into a stout shepherd lad yet."

Chapter Six
At the Sign of the Kicking Pony

Fleet Nigel was a thickset, stumpy lad with brilliant red hair framing his bald, tonsured pate. His face was freckled, and when he rolled up his sleeves, his arms were also freckled, right up to the shoulders.

Giles was tall and thin and already looked like a scholar with his lined face and grave demeanor. He came from a family of fishing folk in Barnhome, in the county of Sussex, and his English was freely dotted with French. Unlike Sebastian, who spoke his midlands English and threw in French for effect, Giles spoke the coastal dialect that also served as a trade language with the French. But his Latin was excellent, almost better than John's, and John had already seen enough of the Oxford students to know that he had as much command of Latin as any Master of a hall.

The place where Fleet Nigel led them, called the Kicking Pony, was already crowded with many an Oxford student seeking an additional breakfast or else the companionship of his mates.

There were several tables—which had to be shared sometimes—and the inn could boast a plank floor.

"Now, this is more pleasant!" Sebastian exclaimed as a steaming platter of herring was set before them. "But tell me, somebody, why do the monks and friars hate us?"

"Because King Edward, God bless him, has made Oxford free," Fleet Nigel said, taking a herring from the plate and biting into it.

"Meaning?" Sebastian asked.

"Meaning at Oxford we can say what we believe and try out different ideas without any of those sooty-black friars condemning us all to everlasting perdition."

"The Dominicans," John said. "You mean they are powerless to interfere at Oxford and control what is taught?"

"Aye, and they hate us for it. England herself is a free and pretty pearl that they'd like to get their hands on," Nigel said. "But not us, eh, Giles?"

Giles had been industriously eating herring, but he looked up to nod, and then he said, "The Dominicans have the Inquisition without restraint in other countries, you know. They burn heretics."

"Aye," Sebastian said with a grim nod.

"I had heard that but not known it for sure," John said. "Though I knew that the Dominicans had been commissioned to keep the Church pure."

"Aye, they'll burn a man for heresy," Giles said. "My father, he knew some of the folk in France who were killed *en masse,* fifty at one time, I think. Their tiny village was set on fire, and the French soldiers drove them back into the flames. Not one escaped. All done at the command of the Dominicans, with the authority of the pope behind them."

"All this, in the name of the merciful Saviour?" John asked. "What had they professed that was heretical?"

"That a man cannot merit heaven, not even with the sacraments of the Church."

"What?" Sebastian exclaimed. "How did they think a man could get to heaven, then?"

"They believed that the Saviour would save by His own will and power," Giles told them.

"Grace," John interjected.

"Yes, grace."

"Why, if that were true, any dog might be saved," Sebastian said.

"Better to trust in the mercy of Christ than in the pope's indulgence," John muttered, thinking of the hanged man they had seen. Sebastian caught his eye. Nigel, with a knowing wink, nodded.

"I cannot explain it as well as they," Giles replied, faltering for words.

"Yet do you believe those Frenchmen, Giles?" Sebastian asked. My father, careless as he was of religion, began even at that early moment to be awakened by the testimony of those French martyrs.

Giles hesitated. "I—I cannot say. My father was sore perplexed by what he heard of them. So here I am. I have come to study and find out."

"True enough!" Fleet Nigel said heartily. "Hands off to the Dominicans! Here you may read St. Thomas Aquinas, Grosseteste, Bradwardine, Augustine, and Peter Lombard to discover the path to heaven!"

"Those French peasants had only the poor Bible, I suppose," Sebastian observed. "No wonder they were misled."

"Sebastian, my friend, you may err there," John said.

"How so?"

"We shall soon see."

Sebastian looked puzzled, but Fleet Nigel laughed. "John, you are a thinker. The city air has set your thoughts in a whirl."

John smiled. "I do not deny it. I have already confessed to the archer here that I feel like one newly able to see."

"*Ma foi!* It was a very babe I met on the way to the Dark Ferret. But he is hardening himself, I see," Sebastian said.

"What, John, since you are free of the Dominicans, shall you side with these French heretics?" Fleet Nigel asked.

"That I know not," John said. "For I have never heard of them before and likely shall never hear of them again if they are treated thus. But this I do say, that we are under a vow to preserve the honor and glory of Christ. And I have seen much thus far that must make Him weep. It is time indeed to study to show ourselves approved of God."

Giles's eyes blazed in approval of this, but Fleet Nigel gave a hearty laugh, and Sebastian—who had already lost his momentary interest in the things of God—only said, "Aye for you, but for me, I had preferred to be in France now, plying the trade I was born to. By my ten skilled fingers! I can't complain of the company I keep at Oxford, but the very name Aquinas fills my head with a deadly stupor."

"Why, I devour Aquinas!" Fleet Nigel exclaimed. He held up a herring and showed it to Sebastian. "See, here is Aquinas!" So saying, he crammed it into his mouth.

"Now I see your methods," Sebastian said. He pointed to another one on the plate. "And if this be Augustine?"

"We shall swallow him up!" Fleet Nigel cried, dividing it with his knife. In a twinkling, each had taken a half and the fish was gone.

"Clerks at Oxford, you two are hogs at the trough!" John exclaimed, laughing in spite of himself.

Fleet Nigel let out a burp. "Why John, it's the only way I can stomach these scholars!" He and Sebastian roared with laughter. Even grave Giles burst out with a laugh at their antics.

"I may laugh now," Sebastian said, wiping his hand across his mouth. "Today I devour the scholars, yet I think perhaps soon they shall begin to devour me."

Chapter Seven
University Learning

Classes began three days later. The principal of each hall blew on a loud horn just before dawn. Men groaned from every cubicle. There was the stamping of feet and rustling of clothes as tunics and cappas were pulled on. Sleepily, the young clerks stumbled down the steps to the water trough outside. There was much puffing and blowing and splashing as they washed their faces in the cold water that chilly morning and then stumbled back inside.

"Oh, by my ten skilled fingers!" Sebastian groaned. "When is breakfast?"

"After mass and lecture," Fleet Nigel moaned. "We live in a state of penance, I think."

They got their books from the cubicle and made for the chapel. John had to force himself to listen to the mass. He held in his hands the *Sentences* of Peter Lombard and the Latin Vulgate, Jerome's fourth-century translation of the Scriptures into Latin. Both were handwritten manuscripts, smudged in places and with some of the pages torn out. He had purchased them secondhand.

Already he had read some of the contents of each, and his heart was soaring. The first chapter of the Gospel of John was still in his mind: *"In principio erat Verbum, et Verbum erat apud Deum, et Deus erat Verbum—"* (In the beginning was the Word, and the Word was in the presence of God, and the Word was God.)

Here was the place where all the problems could be solved. The Word of God was truth and reality, and it was inextricably linked to Christ. Thus, if a man with reverence and humility knew the Word, he would also in some sense know Christ. England might not be doomed after all for her impiety, her foolish indulgences, her fat and wealthy abbots. For England had the Word—at least in Latin, if not in English.

"You hurry like a man eager to run a race," Fleet Nigel observed as they hurried back to the refectory for their first lecture.

"I am eager," John said.

Sebastian sighed heavily. "For me, I am eager for the trencher. Even that rough bit of black bread would be welcome to my stomach."

Fleet Nigel groaned. "Oh, speak not this soon of food."

The refectory was crowded with men finding places at the table and setting down horns of ink and their quills. The college lecture was given in Latin, and the new clerks began to learn the complicated art of scholasticism's rhetoric.

The Master dictated a question: "Can God create a vacuum?" Then he divided the question up. He defined the nature and attributes of God. Next he explained these attributes while the students took notes in a flurry of scratching pens.

Next the Master defined a vacuum. Then he had to define space and substance. Because not all scholars agreed on the nature of substance, he had to give all of the viewpoints on it and explain each one.

John's head was in a whirl as he wrote, but he had time enough to see that Sebastian and Fleet Nigel—and about half the other new students—were having difficulty following the lecture.

It wasn't that the question itself was difficult—there were only two possible answers. And every student in the room knew the nature of vacuums and the attributes of God.

But it was the subtle logic, the steps that the Master took in singling out each detail of every definition, that puzzled the students, especially those who were not good in their Latin.

Later, as their scanty breakfast was set before them, Sebastian exclaimed, "Day after day of this! I'll not touch purgatory after death, my friends. I have found it here!"

"One might truly become a heretic to escape from this place!" Fleet Nigel groaned.

"I can go over the notes with you," John offered.

"John, if you'll do that, you'll be the best of friends!" Sebastian exclaimed. "Yet, woe is me, *mes amis,* this is not the life I was born to!"

"Worse woe on me!" Fleet Nigel cried. "It *is* the life I was born to. I had thought my Latin good, but I am the crudest illiterate. How fared you, Giles?"

"Seemed a long bit of work," Giles admitted. "But I followed his thoughts and understood him."

"Alas, and when I think of the fair maids, the roast mutton, the golden autumn fields," Sebastian mourned. "And I, who shall never marry, shall never plow the good earth after a few years of winning spoil in France, shall never do anything with these strong hands but sit and molder in this dusty, dank, university—"

"Alas, poor Sebastian," John agreed. "True, you seem built to be a jolly English yeoman. Yet at least you have your bow to shoot at the mark—"

"If not at the French," Fleet Nigel quipped.

"—and thus can pass many a happy hour in the field," John added.

"You seek to comfort me, Father John. But my only comfort shall be to doff this robe for my old tunic. Alas!"

"Even a good bit of beef pie would be a comfort," Fleet Nigel mourned.

"Aye, or one little fistfight, and forget a full scale war!" Sebastian agreed.

"Or the sound, even, of my dear mother's voice," said Nigel, and all looked down for a moment. For all of them, home was far away, and they could not even send letters, for their parents were illiterate.

"Or even to feel her rod again," Sebastian said after a moment. "I would laugh for the joy of it and bid her beat me black and blue."

"Alas," Fleet Nigel agreed. "My sweet mother could scold like a crow, yet now it would be sweet as the robin's song in my ear, if I could but hear it."

"I have ne'er yet felt sunk so low in spirit as I have since coming to this university," Sebastian said. "I marvel that a man's spirit *could* sink this low."

"And to think," Giles added, "we've only been to one lecture!"

Chapter Eight
First Year

October was crisp and then became cold. Soon it was November, and the film of ice over the water trough had to be broken before the clerks could wash in the mornings.

Midwinter came, with the ground frozen as solid as iron. The cubicles were cold, and the halls were cold, and mealtime was cold.

The ranks of the students thinned out. Those who fell hopelessly behind or into serious debt sold their tunics, cappas, hoods, and books and went home.

The men from the orders and the seculars jibed at each other, and they found that time did not make their tempers any sweeter. Fights broke out whenever too many members of each group met in the town. These fights were usually broken up, and the professors thundered down warnings to all of the students to behave.

Sebastian may have mourned not having any wars, but he certainly had his fill of fistfights. The burly archer could wade into any crowd of monks, his big fists swinging. A punch from Sebastian Ayleton would drop a mule, and it was just as bad to be grappled by him. He once picked up a big young Dominican who had been a farm boy and threw him clean across the backs of a team of horses and into a water trough. (It was a story he often told me with great relish. "Ho ho!" he would say. "I baptized that one whether he would or no!")

The younger members of the religious orders learned to avoid him. John had little use for fights, and he was wrapped up in his books much more than he was concerned with the grievances of the orders and the seculars against each other. All the same, he was unafraid of any man and could never be persuaded to get out of the way of a man looking for trouble.

"You're still but a stripling in build," Sebastian told him. "But you behave as though you were a giant, Johannes. Pray, give in when bullied. For if you get your head split open, then I am lost. You carry the brains for both of us."

The Kicking Pony was "safe" for seculars, not being a place frequented by the students from the orders. In the spring, Sebastian's father sent word for Sebastian to stay at Oxford, but he also sent him a purse full of French gold. The result was many suppers at the Kicking Pony that the four friends shared.

A steaming hot meat pasty was the very thing for the hungry students after a day's work and the meager supper which Fleet Nigel continued to call their evening penance.

Indeed, after a long winter of poverty at Oxford, all four of the young men looked gaunt and hollow-eyed.

"Still, hunger is the best sauce," Sebastian said with a grin at John. "Eat first, and then pleasant talk afterward, as we have not had for many an evening."

None of them liked to talk about their first days at Oxford, for they were all painfully aware of how rustic and crude they had been. But at last, at one of their suppers at the Kicking Pony, Fleet Nigel said, "How now, John? Not long ago at this very table you promised to learn enough to solve the ills that beset us poor holy men. And only yesternight I heard you disputing with your cousin about the Scriptures."

John blushed. "Forgive me, friends. I was a brash fool to think I could solve all the ills in this world."

Sebastian waved it away. "Come, I have my dreams, John, of conquering France all alone. 'Twas a good thing to wish to uphold mercy and truth."

"Aye!" said Giles.

"That I still seek to do," John told them. "And I will say this: that though I have great love for Peter Lombard and Augustine, and great taste for Aquinas and all the other Church Fathers and great scholars, yet I say they do not touch the Holy Scriptures for truth."

The three others glanced at each other and back at John.

"Come," John said, "Do the Scriptures not claim to be perfect?"

Sebastian and Fleet Nigel shrugged, but Giles said, "Aye, they do. That is why we rely on the wisdom of the Church Fathers. We dare not trust ourselves."

"But the Fathers were as imperfect as we," John argued.

"John!" Sebastian exclaimed. "Think you that Augustine was as great a fool as you or me?"

"I said naught about him being a fool, Sebastian. I only said he was not a perfect man. Answer me: If Augustine and Scripture shall disagree on any point, which shall we choose?"

"They do not disagree," Giles ventured.

"We cannot know that until we study more," John said.

"John, John," Fleet Nigel said. "All this you say because we must study Scripture now as young undergraduates. But when we rise to study the Fathers and Aquinas and Lombard, you shall be equally in love with them." Fleet Nigel was only an average student, but he was loyal to the Church and to Oxford. As any clerk at Oxford will tell you, they did not study Scripture for the sake of Scripture. Rather they studied what the Church Fathers said about Scripture. The Church's commentaries on the Bible were everything, and God's Word was nothing.

"I have privately read much of the Fathers, and they are still but men," John said. "But Scripture comes from God."

"Did God not send the Church Fathers to us?" Fleet Nigel asked, somewhat hotly. "How would you have the Church interpret Scripture without the writings of the Church Fathers?"

John Wycliffe looked evenly at Fleet Nigel and said. "I would let every man who can read, read the Scripture—in English."

"What?" Nigel asked, aghast.

"John!" Sebastian cried.

"And I would have learned men read the Scripture to unlearned men, that all might hear the Scripture," John added. "In English."

"Your soul will burn in hell for that!" Nigel cried. "Would you put the Bible into the hands of a dirty pig farmer? Would you let any fool read it?"

"Many a fool reads it even now, Nigel!" John exclaimed. "Many a fat abbot and an unworthy bishop and I know not what else! They read it and mishandle it!"

Fleet Nigel could only sputter. "Common people cannot be trusted with Scripture! They need it explained to them! Why, would you have women hearing it, too?"

"I would give the Scripture to any creature with an immortal soul!" John told him. "No matter how poor he be, no matter how wretched. For every man must care for his soul. And every woman, too."

"Bah! What do stupid peasants know of their souls?" Nigel asked. "This is the maddest talk I've ever heard."

"Scripture says otherwise," John told him. "The plain Scripture warns every man to look to his soul and cry for wisdom from God and God alone."

"How dare you ignore the Fathers!" Nigel cried and jumped up. "Was not Augustine as suddenly and as abruptly converted as St. Paul? Was there not evidence of the miraculous in that?"

"But Augustine did not claim to be a part of Scripture," John argued. "You are blind if you do not see it, Nigel. And a blind leader of the blind you shall be if you dispense with the Word of God!" He jumped to his feet, too. "How well you talk of fools! Open your eyes to the misery around us!"

"You take an inexperienced position and defend it as a doctor!" Nigel cried.

"Peace, friends, peace!" Giles exclaimed. "Fleet Nigel, in truth! Why do you play the theologian so briskly? Just last night you played the dice. And John, think as you will, but I pray you, speak softly to your friend. He spoke a valid point, and he is not blind. We are all young students."

John Wycliffe seemed almost beside himself with anger. For a moment he and Nigel stared at each other, and everything else in the Kicking Pony was silent. After a moment, both young men sat down.

"I cry your forgiveness," John said. "My wicked temper waxed hot, Nigel."

"It is forgiven, John—let us be friends," Nigel agreed, though his freckled cheeks were red—either from anger or shame—for a jibe from John Wycliffe went hard on one who had to struggle with his studies.

Sebastian tried to ease things with a joke. "In truth, John, after only six months you've made a bold judgment. What shall you find after a year or two years? All England shall not contain it."

"As any learned man can see, England contains many a gross error and deception now," Giles said. "It is a marvel to see all that she will contain, what with the representatives of Christ rolling in wealth and oppressing the poor. And then there are the pardoners selling indulgences to unholy people, the friars walking boldly into houses to take food and other things, and the bishops of England and France fighting each other on the battlefield with sword and lance."

"And, saying that, do you still not see that we must return to the Scriptures solely?" John asked. "These offences have come by men following human wisdom, not the wisdom of God."

"Come, John, not Augustine nor Chrysostom nor Polycarp would have favored these abuses," Giles said, naming off some of the Church Fathers.

"But parts of their writings were misread to lay foundations for these abuses," John suggested. "This nonsense of indulgences and worshiping relics has no foundation in Scripture."

Giles looked down. "That may be the truth." They had all seen the pardoners and some friars hawking relics to the common people, claiming to have such things as a splinter from the pardoned thief's cross, a lock of hair from St. Frideswyde, a piece of bone from Baalam's donkey, all of which were thought to impart special blessings to their owner.

For Fleet Nigel and Sebastian, they doubted that the relics they saw were genuine. But they supposed that a genuine relic might impart blessings. In private, John had told my father, Sebastian, that he doubted that any relic, false or genuine, was good for anything. As yet he had no proof, but he was—thus far—sure that Scripture provided no basis for the veneration of relics.

Sebastian sat back and burped. "There's naught like a big meal for an empty belly, hey messmates? It's even better than cracking a Franciscan on his fat head."

The others relaxed and their talk began to run into safer channels. But Giles briefly glanced at John. "I believe you," he said softly. "*Sola Scriptura.* (Scripture alone.) But I cannot prove it."

John nodded and looked down at his hands. "I can," he said, so softly that only my father, Sebastian, heard him. "Someday, I will." And for the first time, Sebastian Ayleton's carnal heart was touched with the thought that John Wycliffe might be right.

Chapter Nine
The Wrath of God Falls on England
Summer, 1348

Summer and autumn, winter and spring: another year, and then a third. The four who had shared a cubicle their first year had to go their separate ways. John stayed at Balliol Hall. Sebastian, ever furnished with more money from his father, moved into a hostelry where the food and bedding were better. Yet he still relied on John to help him with his studies. Fleet Nigel managed to afford better quarters in Balliol, and Giles qualified for a scholarship at Merton College, several streets away from Balliol.

Giles and John often attended the same lectures, for they were advancing swiftly through such subjects as rhetoric, logic, astronomy, physics, philosophy, and mathematics. They were both well read on Aristotle, and each had fenced words with his classmates in formal *disputation*.

The disputation was a method of argument that used the scholastic system of breaking a question down into its many parts and defining each of the parts. It was rather like running up and down the staircase of logic, Sebastian had once observed, and carrying too many bundles in your arms each way.

I have been told that at some universities in Europe, the disputations are carried out with great politeness and courtly manners. It was not so at Oxford. When two men disputed with each other, everyone else in the class would quickly take sides and immediately start throwing insults back and forth.

"Sit on the secular, friend monk!" some would call if John were disputing a man from the orders. "That will squash him!"

"Ho, stripling, you are delirious from fasting!"

"There is a hole in your robe!"

It was not unusual for the disputations to turn into confrontations. Sometimes wooden stools and inkhorns flew back and forth, as well as insults.

Giles, who was by nature shy, often stumbled during disputations. He would lose strands in his complicated webs of logic, forget a minor point he had been bent on making, or would blush scarlet and falter to a stop when somebody punned or made fun of his arguments.

John, on the other hand, was the champion of his classmates. He liked nothing more than to grapple with the problems in any question set before him. Nor had he ever given up his belief that the Bible, and only the Bible, is the final authority of the Church. In fact, he had convinced a few of his classmates of his position, including Giles. Both the young men were drawing nearer to examinations for the bachelor's degree.

But on this day in late August, Giles and John had their minds fixed on a problem that could not be solved by disputation. The Pestilence that had wracked Europe with death ever since spring had at last set its deadly foot on English soil.

Within seven days of the first signs of sickness in the small port town of Malcombe Regis, not a soul was left alive there. A few people had fled, but everyone else had died.

"We are doomed," Giles said. "It will not spare England."

They were on their way from the chapel to the fair to buy books.

"Hush," John said. "Some here are so frightened they would wring your neck for speaking that prophecy, Giles."

"What think you, John? Is God judging us?"

"So they say. Or perhaps it is truly one of the plagues that will end the world." John shrugged his thin shoulders and saw that Giles's face was chalky white. "What is it? Do you fear death?"

"Sebastian and Fleet Nigel, they be hale and stout men. But you and I be sickly and pale. Alas, when it finds us, it shall kill us on the first sweep."

"True, it is likely. Yet every man must die sometime."

Giles looked down. John waited but as his friend did not speak at all, John said softly, "Why do we fear death, Giles? You in your heart and I in mine believe the same thing."

Giles glanced up. "What is that?"

"Come. You have read St. Paul. The saving of the soul comes from God, not the Church. Indeed, He foreknew His people before they were born, Giles. It is a matter between man and God. The Church has no say in it."

"I have hoped so," Giles confessed. "I have prayed so, John. For I trust that if it were in God's hands, that I could then have hope. But if it all rested on my merits, I know that hell will open its mouth and catch me."

"Perhaps even this contrition on your part is a sign of His grace at work in you. Have hope." John grasped Giles by the hand. "I cannot help you, for I cannot determine the state of your soul, friend Giles; yet I bid you look to the Saviour. He is merciful."

"Thank you, John. You have helped. May God help us to bear the horror that comes."

In the weeks that followed, the Pestilence crept steadily up the River Stour, taking one town after another, and then it came down the River Thames toward Oxford. News came of the symptoms of the plague: a painful swelling under the arm or in other parts of the body, the appearance of gray blotches, profuse sweating, fever, and finally death. The Pestilence was not unknown in England, but it had never been so common. It had killed by the dozens before, but now it was killing by thousands.

And then it took a new form. A man might be walking or working or at his prayers and then suddenly collapse with fever. He would die before the gray blotches had a chance to appear. A man could get up in the morning well and be dead before supper.

St. Mary's church at the university was crowded with supplicants day after day, and in the town, St. Martin's was also filled. Yet the Pestilence came to Oxford.

Lying on his pallet at night, John would hear some of the others crying in their sleep, dreaming that they had the Pestilence. Then they would awake, and he would hear the sobs of relief mingled with terror. But then there came a time when the cries were not those of one leaving a nightmare but of entering it and finding it real.

"Johannes! Johannes! Mercy, I pray. Bring me water. I swear I will not look on you nor touch you," one, Nicholas Bates, called out to him one day. The younger man lay outside his cubicle, drenched in sweat.

John knelt by him. "You should be in the hospital, Nicholas!"

The younger man shook his head. "No room—no room, Johannes. We are left." He began to sob. "Left! Left to die!"

"I am here. I will gladly fetch you water," John said.

"Say an *Ave* for me, Johannes. On the way."

"Nicholas, I counsel you now to consider carefully the Saviour and the cross."

"Oh, water, John. Give me water."

"Of course. I shall run."

He darted down the hall, but when he came rushing back with pail and dipper, Nicholas was dead.

John stood staring at him. He later told me of that moment of fleshly horror of death. *I touched him,* he thought. *I breathed the same air he breathed.* Fear of the Pestilence swept over him with a freezing chill. But the laments of the dying lad rang in his ears: *"Left! Left to die!"*

"Oh Lord, I vow, until You smite me dead with this, I shall not spurn any. Dear Saviour, help me not to falter in fear. Deliver me from the pride of life. Amen."

He turned and took the pail away, and then he came back and took Nicholas's hands in his, raised the arms, and stooped down with his back to the dead boy. He drew the arms over his shoulders, so that Nicholas's head rested against his own hair and the back of his neck. Then he stood up, so that Nicholas was carried on his back, almost piggyback, the way the farmers carried their children when they romped. In that fashion, he carried the lad out to bury him.

Before the week ended, Oxford shrank to a ghost town. The professors fled; the Masters fled; the friars and monks— most of them—fled. Yet even as they fled, some of them stumbled and fell, struck down. A man in the act of mounting his horse could be taken. To be out of the town gates was no guarantee of safety.

"Where do they think to hide from it?" Sebastian asked John one September afternoon as they watched the line of people fleeing the town.

"They have country retreats; they have homes . . . so what? I care not what the doctors say. No place is safe." Sebastian spoke as one trying to convince himself.

"You will not go home?" John asked.

"Nay, my father bid me stay for fear I die by the roadside. And you?"

"The same. What of Fleet Nigel and Giles?"

"Giles has gone to die with his family or die on the way. Fleet Nigel found service with the Bishop of London's entourage. He sent me word and asked to bid you goodbye.

They have gone out to the country to escape it. Just like a bishop—run when danger comes!"

"Yet nobody forced Nigel to go with him," John observed. "The bishop is not the only one who has fled."

Sebastian hung his head. After a moment he said, "I would have gone too, John, if I'd had the chance."

"God may spare or smite, Sebastian. But if we die, let us die like Christian men. Let us stay and do what we can."

Chapter Ten
The Fiery Furnace

It did not end in one year but stretched out to two. Following the prescribed methods of precaution, the townsmen lit bonfires wherever possible and threw on sweet-smelling woods such as pine or juniper or used incense to purify the air.

There was no more time for last rites, funeral orisons, or private graves. John and Sebastian, like any other able-bodied man, were conscripted to dig mass graves, to build fires, to seek out the dead, and to help the Watch guard against burglary in the vacant buildings, though the burglary ran on apace in spite of the Watch.

Because they were deacons, John and Sebastian did their best to remember to mumble a final benediction over the dead: *"Requiem aeternam dona eis, Domine."* (Eternal rest give them, Lord.)

When John had time to think, he found himself debating with nobody in particular whether this was the end of the world.

Word came weeks later that Sebastian's mother had died. Then John found out months too late that both his parents were dead. Thomas Bradwardine, a controversial professor who was at odds with the pope, also died. Bishop and archbishop, knight and squire, shepherd and farmer, monk and friar—all were vulnerable to it. The pope, because he refused to see anybody at all throughout the duration of the Pestilence and remained secluded in his marble walls, lived. In Oxford, the dead lay in doorways or in the midst of the streets. Those fortunate enough to die in their beds were hauled away every morning and evening.

Food was scarce and expensive in the town of Oxford. Even if there had been food, few people could have afforded to buy anything. John often was able to haggle for a meal.

It was a lonely and hard life. My father, Sebastian Ayleton, would rarely speak of this part of his youth. And John Wycliffe never spoke of the Pestilence at all, nor did he ever write about it. Yet it was there—and it was that great event that shaped both men. The years of death and misery touched my father's hard heart more than any preaching had ever done—that much he admitted to me. It was during the Pestilence that he came to question the Church and to seek both comfort and counsel from John Wycliffe.

And John Wycliffe became more and more convinced of God's grace and power to save souls. With every passing day he came to disagree more and more with the Mother Church.

In his free time he searched out those who were suffering and calling for a priest. Priests were rare indeed, for many had died and those who had not would often refuse to go near a sick person. John went and did what he could.

"Ah, only a deacon," said one sick man whom John found lying in a doorway on a bundle of rags. "What can you do? You have no sacrament to give me."

"I can bid you look to the Saviour," John said. "Even as the thief on the cross did, for he also died cut off from men and yet pitied by God."

"How you talk."

"But it is so, my friend. He mourned for his sins and Christ promised to take him to Paradise."

"I shall confess to you."

"I will hear you," John agreed. "But only Christ can forgive you. I shall help you, if I can, to bring your sins before Him."

The man lay still; whether in a delirium or fatigued or in the throes of death, John did not know. But at last he spoke in a whispering, hoarse voice. "I had five children and a wife, and all are dead, all gone but me. And the last two had no priest. The very youngest had not e'en been baptized. She shall not see the face of God, poor sweet thing that she was."

"No, I am persuaded that she shall," John said. "For God tells us that He loves children. Did not Jesus bid the children come to Him and be blessed? And you, I am persuaded, if you will ask mercy of God, He will show you mercy and you shall see your child in heaven."

"God have mercy on my soul. I have not kept the Sabbaths. I—" His voice became less audible, and John bent closer to catch the words.

"John, I've found you," Sebastian's voice said from behind him just then. The stout archer was carrying a bag of food.

"I cannot come, Sebastian," John said. "I must stay with him."

"Ah, I thought it was a corpse. Shall I offer him a bit of milk? I have some here."

John glanced at Sebastian and nodded. He turned back to the sick man and said, "Nay. Nay, Sebastian. He is dead."

Sebastian's voice became gentler. "Come on, then," he said after a pause. "Like as not we shall join him shortly."

He helped John up. The two looked wearily at each other. Sebastian had wide streaks of soot down his cheeks, and there were ashes in his hair. He had been tending the fires.

A pall of smoke hung over everything, and smoky billows rolled down the streets like fog. From some building nearby they could hear the bang-banging of a pillager breaking into a shop to get his fill of stolen goods.

"Where did you get milk?" John asked. "How did you get a whole bag of food?"

"Purchased, John. I purchased them. Come. It may be our last meal together. Let us go to my room and eat it."

"You are deep in melancholy, Sebastian. Even through all this I have never seen you so grim and gloomy."

Sebastian glanced sideways at him as they half walked and half staggered up the narrow street. "I may as well tell you plainly. I can think of no fair way to cloak what I must say. Fleet Nigel is dead."

John's face did not really change. He could no longer be shocked by the sudden news of death. "So," he said at last in a quiet voice. "He has died." Neither said anything until John asked, "He was not alone, I hope?"

"I know not. It happened months and months ago, not long after he had set out."

"Yes, I see."

News traveled slowly even when times were good, and during the plague it was haphazard and slow. Both men had often wondered about the fate of Fleet Nigel and Giles, and now John's thoughts turned to Giles for a moment, and he wondered if his premonition of death had come to pass.

"We shall soon join Fleet Nigel, John," Sebastian said.

"I doubt it not, yet I find it hard to fear or even wonder about it any more. More are leaving this world than staying in it. And those who stay often do it at the cost of abandoning their own children and beloved ones to escape the look or touch of death."

They came at last to Sebastian's hostelry and wearily climbed the ladder to his room. It was a plain room with a chimney and grate, and the only furniture was a mattress on the floor.

Sebastian opened the bag and took out bread, cheese, onions, and a small crock of milk which he had been careful not to spill. He folded the cloth sack and set it in a corner.

"How did you come by so much food?" John asked.

Sebastian glanced at him. "I'll tell you, but you'll not like it. Yet I counsel you think twice before you refuse it, John."

"Say on, I will hear you out."

"When I carry a dead man who has been deserted by all, before I throw him into the grave, I say the *requiem* over him, pray for his pardon, and search his pockets for coins."

John had sunk onto the mattress, but now he leaped up, horrified. "Grave robbery!" he cried.

"It is not grave robbery," Sebastian said wearily. "For he's not in the grave, and were his family there, I would have to do it anyway and give the coins to his widow. And what would you I do? Throw the coins in with him? Will they resurrect with the body, John? Will they get his soul past St. Peter into heaven?"

"Of course not!"

"Well, from whom have I done the theft? It was not his will nor his family's will that he be buried with coins in his pocket. And I am the last to do him service—service for which the priest would normally be paid. And I do this service whether a man has coins or not."

"True, true," John agreed and sat down again, too exhausted to stay standing.

"Mayhap I should not do it," Sebastian said. "So that you and I could conveniently starve and be of no help to anyone."

"The point is well taken, Sebastian!" John exclaimed, irritated at the sarcasm. "I have no argument. Let us eat and be done with it!"

They ate in silence. John had no memory of lying back on the mattress, but when he next opened his eyes, the shutters were thrown open, and the sky outside was flushed with the pink dawn. Sebastian—who must have slept on the floor— stood looking out on the dismal town. He thrust his feet into his shoes.

"I took your bed!" John exclaimed, standing up. "Forgive me."

Sebastian grinned at him. "No offense taken, John. You were welcome to it."

They looked at each other a little sheepishly, both ashamed at how close they had come to losing their tempers the night before.

"Well," Sebastian said at last. "We have lost our Fleet Nigel and have not heard a word of Giles in over a year. But I shall stand by you, John, come what may, until this Pestilence be past or we be dead."

"Aye, and I by you, Sebastian. You have ever stood by me," John said warmly.

"And yet—" Sebastian said.

"Yes?"

"We are older men now, John. And we have stared long and hard at the face of Death."

"Truth, Sebastian."

The big archer looked away. "I know now that I cannot be a priest. Not at all."

"Why not?"

"Think ye what ye will, John. But if life be short and the end bitter, as we have seen, I vow I will live and die an English yeoman. I will marry and have children—I take it as a holy vow. Nay, don't laugh. I want blue sky over my head and the song of birds in my ears," Sebastian said. "And if I die young, I pray it will be with a French arrow in my breast and my comrades around me. But if I live to old age, it will be with a good stout wife and many stout children at my knee."

John turned away.

"You laugh!" Sebastian cried.

"No," John said. "I weep." He sat at the edge of the mattress and put his face in his arm. "I must weep. Now."

"John, forgive me. It was no time to speak of leaving my only friend."

"I take no heed of that. I weep because I want it for you. Go and marry. And may God grant that all this be but a fable in the ears of your children." He brought his tears under control and looked at Sebastian. "When will you leave?"

"Not until this is over, if God grant that I live through it. I must try to convince my father, if he live. And if he die, I shall be master of his house and will choose for myself."

"It is a good thing you were poor in Latin, Sebastian, else you might be a priest already and 'twould be too late," John said with a shaky laugh.

Sebastian grinned. "I'm slower than you, John Wycliffe, but smart enough perhaps to drag my feet knowingly when I am marched where I would not go. If I lived at Oxford twenty years, I think I would find a way to put off ordination."

Chapter Eleven
Safety Again

In the winter of 1350, a group of flagellants visited the town of Oxford and began their procession outside the doors of St. Martin's.

Marching in rows, stripped to the waist, each one armed with a short knotted whip, they made a procession before the church door. "From thy fearsome pestilence," half of them cried.

"Good Lord deliver us!" the others answered. And in rhythm to their chanting, every second man struck the back of the man in front of him with his whip. The last line would march to the front, and the ordeal would be continued until every man's back was a mangled mass of blood and broken flesh.

"I can bear no more," John said to Sebastian. "Let us go before they trample each other."

"See the townspeople," Sebastian said as they hurried back to the hostelry. "They think the beaters do great good. The merits of their tortures are said to have moved God to abate the plague."

"And do you believe that, my friend?"

"Nay. If God be pleased so by our torment, He need not have abated the plague at all."

"They do blaspheme God by presuming that such torture would please Him. Do they take Him to be Baal, a drinker of man's blood?" John asked.

There were still deaths every day at Oxford, but not nearly so many as there had been, perhaps only one or two a day. Yet the town was sorely depopulated, and law and order had not been completely restored. Townspeople had moved into Balliol Hall and made themselves at home, and Sebastian had persuaded John to stay with him. Life was counted very cheap in the aftermath of all the deaths, and Sebastian thought it possible that some of the uninvited guests at Balliol might resent John overmuch.

Indeed, cut throats and broken heads seemed much more common than they ever had been in Oxford's narrow streets. More than once in the last several weeks, Sebastian and John had pulled brawlers apart in the street. And trying to get a meal in peace was also nearly impossible, for if they were at a public house, a fight or an argument nearly always broke out somewhere in the house, and if they were at their room, they would hear some disturbance outside.

"Marry, 'twill be good to see some decent Oxford gowns sweeping through the streets again," Sebastian said as they went up High Street near Queen's Hall and then turned around again when they saw a band of surly townsmen lounging on the front steps. Sebastian sighed. "We'll have to go 'round the long way, I suppose, to get out the east end of town. These townsmen are enough to give a man the cramp."

"I suppose they will settle down once a new term begins," John mused.

"Once we get a decent crew of constables and the Watch is reorganized," Sebastian added. "Honest fear of a good whipping will settle them."

"Still, we could go through," John mused, looking back. "They ought not behave as though they owned the street."

"John Wycliffe, as I've told you oft enough, you mustn't have your brains knocked out, however worthy the cause. You'll serve many a better cause with your brains safe inside your head."

"If this land were but under true Christian instruction, we need never have feared either Pestilence or violence," John said.

"Ah, you sing that song again!" And Sebastian gave a chuckle.

"You may laugh," John said, "knowing it is my pet theory. Yet only last night you were talking of Giles and bemoaning the Pestilence and the robbers and cutpurses who freely haunt the roads. Would the English Church but return to the innocence of the early church, God would spare us these chastenings."

Sebastian had become sober at the mention of Giles. "Truth, John," he admitted. "When I think of him among the ravening Pestilence or the rogues who would kill him for a penny, I greatly fear. If Fleet Nigel did not survive, how could Giles?"

"And yet you and I are both alive and hale, and we have looked on and even touched both the sick and the dead."

"I try to hope to see him again. He was a fair scholar, like you, and too nobly good to be taken so young."

"Truth, but look, who is that waving on Carfax?" John asked, and pointed to the town square.

"He sports a cappa! John, the man himself! It is Giles!"

"Nay, it's too small and stooped for Giles."

"As we've spoken, God has sent him, John!" Sebastian cried, running up to the square. "It is! It is!"

John went running after the big archer. As he drew closer, he saw that it was Giles, a Giles now aged as though ten years had passed.

"Giles! Our brother Giles!" And Sebastian threw his bear-like arms around his friend. "You are more welcome than an angel!"

"Dear brother, what a welcome!" Giles said, embracing Sebastian. "But you are thinner, Sebastian. I find a slighter man with a greater heart than when I left. What, John— tears? You ought to be laughing, for my dream of death has not come to pass. It was but morbid fancy's picture that I painted."

He and John embraced and looked at each other. There were gray strands in Giles's hair, and—if possible—his face was more lined than it had been before.

"Can we be lads of twenty or twenty-one?" Giles asked. "We be old men, by our looks and tears."

"Say naught of age," Sebastian said. "I feel as though life were about to begin anew."

"How fared your families?" Giles asked, looking from the big archer to the small scholar.

Sebastian shook his head. "Brother John is an orphan, and I have lost my sweet mother."

"But yours?" John asked.

"All well, thank God. My dear father and I talked oft and long as God allowed us. Indeed, our whole street where our house and shop are situated was but lightly touched. While, two streets over, only four souls survived at all." He looked from one to the other. "And Fleet Nigel? Has he come back?"

"Nay," Sebastian began and stopped.

"I dreamed of him, standing in the marshes outside of town all alone. It pierced my heart to see him so—yet I'd hoped 'twas but another morbid fancy," Giles mourned. "Alas, did he die alone?"

John shook his head. "None can tell. He was with the bishop's retinue. Yet I would take little thought of sorrowing dreams, Giles. For many were bound to die in the Pestilence, and certainly many of those played a part in all our dreams."

" 'Twas too much to hope we should all be preserved," Giles said at last. "But it seems to be ending at last. Have the doctors come back?"

"Nay," John said. "I fear we may have a long wait. Funds are low, many have died and must be replaced, and many are caught in settling inheritances."

"But we may study, at least," Giles said. "And I hunger to hear your thoughts, friend John. We shall practice our disputations and all three judge one another, eh?"

"I shall practice at the longbow," Sebastian said. "And you two shall judge each other. If the term be postponed again, I shall make the most of it."

Chapter Twelve
The Town-Gown Riot
Autumn, 1353

Two more years passed. John Wycliffe and Giles of Barnhome, both twenty-three years of age, at last renewed their preparations to receive the Bachelor's degree. Lectures had begun again at Oxford, four years after the fear of the Pestilence had driven the professors away.

Sebastian continued at his studies. But his spare time was taken up in selecting a maid to ask for in marriage or in composing a letter to his father announcing his desires to give up the priesthood and go back to archery.

As he later admitted to me, not many a man wished his daughter to marry one so likely to be both penniless and away at war. And Sebastian, brave as any man in battle, was finding it difficult to face his father—even in a letter. The months stretched out, with no progress up either avenue.

John and Giles stood for their examinations and passed them, thus earning the Bachelor's degree. Their next climb would be to the Master of Arts in three years, and from thence to the Bachelor of the sacred page, or Bachelor of Theology. But it would be a long way to that high point, for most of the seculars, after receiving the Master of Arts and ordination into the priesthood, left Oxford to take a parish.

"Perhaps by the time you are Masters, I shall be a Bachelor," Sebastian said with a laugh as they gathered round a joint of mutton at the Kicking Pony.

"Indeed, Sebastian, perhaps by then you will have found a maid who will take you," John quipped, and Giles laughed.

"You strike unfairly where I am wounded, John," Sebastian said, trying to smile at the jibe. "Alas! What ails these Oxford maids! Many a Leicester girl would have jumped to marry Sebastian Ayleton."

"If you but gain your father's permission, all will be well," Giles predicted.

"Aye, there's the mark you must shoot for, Sebastian," John agreed. "From what I hear, the maids like you well enough, but their fathers must also be pleased. And it takes a farm and an inheritance to please Oxford yeomen."

"You may say so," Sebastian agreed. "But 'twould be easier to win my father's permission if I had but a wife to show him to prove I could be no priest. What now?" And he turned at a commotion across the room. Two townsmen were going it hammer and tongs with the legs from their stools, hitting each other.

"Why does no one stop them!" Giles cried, jumping up.

The innkeeper came rushing near them—but not too near—"Friends, friends, this is a peaceful house!" he cried.

"All merely watch! Come!" John exclaimed. Just then one man knocked the other so hard on the head that the second fell, stunned.

The three scholars pushed their way through the standing knot of people. The standing combatant raised the stout stick to strike again, and Sebastian grabbed his arm. "Don't strike a fallen man—not while Sebastian Ayleton stands on his two good legs!" the archer cried.

"Be off, loutish knave!" one of the onlooking townsmen cried. "This was no concern of yours!"

"What, would you have murder done in this man's house?" John asked, standing by the innkeeper. "It looks like this one had thought to kill his comrade."

Giles knelt by the stunned fighter. "God is merciful. This one lives," he said.

"Clerk, you have laid hands on a dangerous man," the first man said to Sebastian. "Let me go."

"Drop the stave, else I break you on my knee if I must," Sebastian exclaimed.

"Rush him, you fools!" the man cried to the townsmen.

But there were other clerks in the room. One snatched up a cleaver from a table. "Stay off!" he warned the townsmen.

The innkeeper put his head in his hands. "Alas! Peace to all!" he cried.

"Are you mad?" John asked the clerk. "Set the blade aside." He looked at the angry cluster of townspeople. "We meant no harm but to save the life of this poor man. Sebastian, release that one, I pray you. And you, friend, think twice before you kill for the sake of mere words."

Sebastian obeyed John. Two of the townsmen pushed Giles aside and picked up their fallen comrade. The attacker glanced fiercely at the three scholars. "Sweetly you preach, by the mass! It turns my stomach. How long shall we have to bear with you Oxford clerks?"

"Of a surety, no more this night," John promised. "This man's peaceful house has been put into enough danger. We shall go, but shame to you, for behaving thus!"

"Take that back, clerk!" the attacker cried, and brandished the stool leg as though he would club John.

"Great wrong has been done!" John said hotly. And he glared hard at his would-be assailant.

"I *knew* I should have broke him on my knee," Sebastian muttered.

"Alas! You'll ruin me yet!" the innkeeper cried. The townsmen surged closer until the three scholars were all closed in. Giles stood up beside John.

"We shall go in peace," Giles said to the angry man. "I pray you, cause no more uproar. Not in this good man's house where all of us have enjoyed such hospitality."

"True," Sebastian added. "If there needs be a fight, at least let us all pass outside into the street and spare our host."

The man lowered his club. "Go, clerks, out of my sight before I forget myself again."

"Come," John said. He saw Sebastian's reluctance and added, "For the sake of our host."

The three clerks left, and the other clerks also paid their scores and left.

"There would have been a nasty bit of work," Giles said when they were out on the cool, dim street.

"You may say so," Sebastian agreed. "By my ten skilled fingers! I have ne'er seen such bloodlust, I, who've kept company with the roughest of soldiers."

"One might forget the orders and seculars in the face of these mobs of townsmen," Giles observed. "I ne'er saw this degree of hostility in a friar or monk. Does it come because we forced people out of the halls and back to their own houses?"

"Who can say?" John asked. "There have been fights between us before, but never have I seen such antagonism. Yet it was one of our members that took up the knife, remember."

"Truth, but the lad was frightened," Sebastian said.

"Nevertheless, cooler heads had best prevail, else blood will be shed," John said.

Winter passed, and the Pestilence seemed altogether vanished. The spring and summer were mild. John earned what he could by tutoring and by assisting at lectures. His parents' farm had passed to his older brother, yet there had been some money settled on him, which at last came to him. He used it for his tuition and books. The autumn term began.

But there was a restlessness over the university and town. The Kicking Pony was still open to Oxford seculars, and the food was just as good and the innkeeper's welcome just as cheerful. But there was talk that some of the cheaper lounging places for students were charging higher prices for poorer food and drink. It was harder for new clerks to get a decent room in town or to pay a fair price for used books. Ever since the Pestilence had ended, the townsmen seemed much less friendly to the students.

All the same, the surface of Oxford seemed calm enough. The law was enforced and the courts were fair. Cold winter set in, and the new year came as fair as any other.

The feast day of St. Scholastica was a free day to the Oxford students. After morning mass, John and his two companions visited the St. Giles fair to inspect books. Sebastian was not particularly interested in books, but he went along to see the sights, for the fair was always colorful on a feast day, with the tumblers, jugglers, and sweetmeat sellers.

John had developed a new theory that the Church was truly known only by God and not by man, that—though a man had his name on the Church roll—a man's membership in the true Church depended on his relationship with God.

"This makes my head spin," Sebastian said.

"It is simple for one who reads the Scripture," John retorted.

"I think I follow it," Giles said. "For Jesus said that not all who call him Lord should see heaven or in any sense truly be known by Him. John concludes, then, that while men accept those who are falsely or vainly crying 'Lord, Lord' in a visible, earthly church, yet God knows such as belong to Him, and that body of believers may be invisible."

"Now I greatly fear," Sebastian said. "For I do begin to understand—what do I hear? Bells!"

"The bells of St. Mary's!" John exclaimed. "A call for help! Is there fire?"

"Nay, even closer ring the bells of St. Martin's!" Giles cried. "It is a fight! Town and gown are at it now!"

Everybody at the stalls and pavilions looked up and stepped back. Townsmen and clerks eyed each other.

"Quick, perhaps we can separate them yet!" John said. "It likely started near Carfax."

The three scholars, hot on the heels of both townsmen and clerks, raced towards the center of town. Before they had reached it, men came streaming out of alleyways and up the narrow streets.

"Too many!" Sebastian cried. "Back, back, friends, around the fair and the long way to Queen's Hall or Balliol. We shall be safe there!"

They turned and pushed against the waves of people milling toward them. Rocks and refuse flew through the air, and the townsmen began clouting them as they tried to force a way through.

"University filth!"

"Run, vermin, before you be squashed!"

Other insults, as well as rocks and trash, were hurled at them as they pushed their way through, and many a blow landed on their shoulders as they went, but it would have been suicide to fight back. All they could do was flee.

"We could be earning sixpence a day for this in France," Sebastian muttered as he led the way and kept his arms around his head. Rocks clattered against the buildings around him.

They pushed through the crowd and found a clear alley where they could pass in single file. But just as they made their way into it, they saw half a dozen Franciscans running toward them, each brandishing a processional crucifix high in the air.

"Do they mean to fight?" Sebastian asked.

Giles looked back. "There comes a band of townsmen behind us!"

The Franciscans rushed toward the three clerks. *"Pax! Pax!"* they cried. *"Pax vobiscum!"*

"They seek to make peace," John said. "Let them pass if they desire."

Sebastian cried out to warn the Franciscans, "Go back! None will listen to you! The mob is on our very heels!"

But the friars pushed past. They thrust the crucifixes down among the mob of townsmen and the few clerks who were being dragged along.

"*Pax vobiscum! Pax vobiscum!*" they cried. "Peace be with you!"

The interruption enabled those clerks caught up in the mob to start fighting back. The townsmen fought both clerks and friars.

It was impossible to get through to Balliol. But the closer they got to the halls, the more university men they saw. Where their own numbers were strong enough, the university men made a good show at beating back the townsmen.

A rock flung through the air glanced off the side of John's head, and he stumbled into Sebastian, dazed. As he later told my father, he knew nothing for several minutes except the sight of the ground spinning by and Sebastian's big feet pumping back and forth. The next thing he knew, Sebastian and Giles had pulled him into a dim hall and set him on a pallet. Had my father Sebastian not acted quickly that day, the world might have lost John Wycliffe.

"Do you know me, John?" the big man asked.

"Aye, it has only dazed me," John said, trying to sit up.

"Nay, keep still," Sebastian said. "We are all three safe in Merton Hall, and shall bide here until this passes."

John fainted or fell asleep, and when he woke up, the hall was dark. "Where am I?" he asked.

"Quiet, lad, quiet," Sebastian's voice said. "We are in Merton Hall and vespers has just passed. Giles has gone to beg you a bit of bread from the refectory."

"My skull rings like a bell."

"Be thankful you were not hurt worse," Sebastian said.

"For that I do thank God. Is all well?"

"Some lectures are canceled for the morrow, I heard. And poor Giles left a book he had just purchased at the fair. But otherwise all seems well. It is quiet outside."

"Sore loss for Giles. That book cost him a good piece of silver."

"Mayhap he can retrieve it tomorrow if the fair was not ruined. Here he is now."

Giles knelt by John. "Well, brother John, I feared we had lost you," Giles said.

"Nay, my skull is too thick to crack," John said with a laugh and hungrily devoured the bread.

Chapter Thirteen
The End of Youth

The next day dawned fair, and the morning passed with no indication of what was about to burst forth.

John did not wake up until long after morning mass. He found Sebastian seated by him, dozing. John slapped the big man on the knee. Sebastian started awake, then smiled.

"How is your skull today?" he asked.

"Quieter. Where has Giles gone?"

"After his precious book. I—" Sebastian cut himself off and leaped up. "What do I hear? John, the bells of St. Mary's are ringing again!"

John struggled to get up, and Sebastian pulled him to his feet.

"The refectory," John gasped. "There is a window there. I can come if you'll help me." For his head ached when he moved.

With John supported on Sebastian's shoulder, the two hurried into the dining room of Merton. They dashed to the unglazed window and looked out. "I hear a cry of murder," Sebastian said. It was that cry, he later told me—with the tears in his eyes—that again cast his mind to God. To God, and to Giles. For he felt in that instant that some dreadful fate had befallen Giles.

"Shutter that window, you fools!" someone within the hall screamed at them. "The townsmen are shooting at Oxford lads!"

Sebastian, heedless of the order, turned to John. "I shall go find Giles."

"And I with you."

"Your head is still bruised."

"I shall not falter, Sebastian. We must both go seek him."

"Very well, but we may both be killed. There are arrows flying, I see. It is much worse than yesterday."

"I fear them not."

They fled the refectory, but the great doors of Merton Hall were closed and barred, and there were students piling stools, tables, anything they could lift, up against the doors.

"What shall we do?" John asked.

"I'll go out the window. You stand by it to get me back in."

"And how shall I do that?" John demanded.

The soldier in my father came to the surface. "Find a rope or make one," he ordered. "Obey in this, John, or we'll be too late."

"As you say, then, only hurry," John agreed.

They went back to the dining room, and Sebastian climbed up on the stone ledge of the windowsill. He had to crouch to fit in the narrow window.

"Is the drop too high?" John asked, unable to peer past him.

"Nay, I shall go full length and reduce it by a good six or seven feet. There is a storeroom somewhere, to keep ropes for the hanging candle racks." So saying, Sebastian lowered himself from the windowsill and dropped safely to the ground below. He held the gown of his robe up and raced toward Carfax.

"God keep you, Sebastian," John called, and he went to find a rope.

That short prayer lingered in my father's heart long after Merton Hall was behind him. He had played the man in the presence of John Wycliffe, but as he raced through the dangerous streets, his heart quaked. He saw a dead Oxford clerk flung against one of the college walls, an arrow sticking out of his back. Around him were the cries of the outraged townsmen, and the answering yells from angry clerks and masters, or else their screams of fear.

In that hour of horror, he later confessed to me, he saw that Sebastian Ayleton was not really the giant he had seemed. He was afraid for his own life and afraid for the life of his friend Giles. He longed to know that God would keep him safe in His hand, and for the first time he keenly realized that he had no true means of approaching God.

Sebastian spent the afternoon hiding and seeking. He sought to stay unseen, yet he forced himself to check all over Oxford for some sight of Giles.

Meanwhile, near the college halls, the fighting and screaming lulled at midday, and the Merton students argued about whether to take down the barricade. More than a few of them dropped out the windows to survey the town.

"Alas, there is murder done," a master named Alan Tonworth said to John. "It shall be worse before 'tis better. The townsmen have done murder and will not be held back by mere unarmed clerks."

"I have friends out there," John lamented. "I should have gone."

"If your friends are wise, they will return before evening," Tonworth advised. "If not by then, you truly may despair of their lives. The night will be violent."

John waited uneasily. Terce was not rung, but about vespers time, the sullen lull was broken by new commotion and the screams of men on the rampage. Sebastian was barely a horse's length ahead of the mob as he raced for Merton Hall.

"John! John! Throw the rope!" he cried.

John had tied the rope to a stout log destined for the fireplace. He set the log across the open window and flipped the end of the rope to Sebastian. The rope grew taut and the log was pulled tight across the window, but the stout wood held.

Sebastian scaled the wall and got one brown hand over the sill. The log fell as Sebastian let go of the rope. John took him under the shoulders and pulled him in.

"We be in sore danger," he gasped. "Alas, I could not find Giles. The mob has gone the other way. Lower the rope for any others who come for help."

But no others came. Another mob of townsmen swirled around Merton, and they flung torches against it, but the walls were solid stone. John pulled the rope up so that none could enter that way. Some of the rioting men pushed against the heavy doors, but the barricade and bars held.

The crowd pressed on, screaming and shouting. Pikes and spears waved in the air, and arrows flew.

"Madness!" Sebastian cried.

"They are bent on killing," John cried. "Pray that Giles is safe!"

"The clerks shut the town gates to keep out the field workers and others," Sebastian told him. "But those outside must have broken them down."

"I smell smoke," John said. They looked out the window and scanned the street.

"They are burning the university," Sebastian said.

The long night passed, heavy with smoke and the occasional sound of fighting. Towards dawn they heard the noise of horses being whipped up. They rushed to the window and saw a group of masters and professors storm toward the gates together, obviously in the hopes of riding down any opposition.

"Go!" Sebastian cheered. "They ride like knights, John!"

"Pray God that they make it," John said. "Or we shall be starved out and killed in our turn before help comes."

Other masters and bachelors crowded around to watch, but the knot of horsemen was soon lost to sight.

"I only pray that they find the gates open," Sebastian said.

"They must have good hopes of it," John guessed. "And I also do, for 'tis unlikely the townsmen so soon repaired what they themselves broke down last night."

"I ought to go seek for Giles," Sebastian said, but he checked himself at sight of a band of townsmen who rushed down the street calling out to each other.

"Nay," John said. "They have done murder. If Giles found good shelter, he is safe, but if they caught him, I know they have killed him."

"Look!" one behind John said, pointing out the window. "All the halls are burning."

"Not all," Sebastian said. "But some, sure enough. Think you that any of us shall escape alive from all this, John?"

"We are in God's hands, and the King's men may be on the way if any got out last night."

They watched the dense cloud of smoke rise billowing to the sky.

"The libraries!" someone cried.

"Alas that they should burn precious books!" another lamented.

"A curse that those rogues did not all perish in the Pestilence!" one of the masters cried.

John glanced at Sebastian and saw the tears that stood in the big man's eyes. "The books, John," Sebastian said. "I had no love for them, but what a loss they have wrought on us!" Both he and John knew the tedious labor it took to produce one book, as well as the high price a student had to pay to get it. A book meant many supperless nights, patching old shoes with straw, doing without firewood and candles, tutoring or dictating by the hour, denying one's self every pleasure and every necessity possible just to save up the coins it took for one book.

Throughout the rest of the day the townsmen ran back and forth, and the smoke hung like a cloud over all. At last, towards the time that terce should be rung in the mid-afternoon, the clear cry of a horn sounded up the street. John, Sebastian, and the others leaped up and looked.

"Those are the King's men!" Sebastian cried. "All together lads!" And the captive scholars let out a loud hurrah through the window.

A mounted captain in glittering mail raced down the street on horseback. Seconds later, footmen, also in mail, hurried along behind him, their spears at the ready, their metal suits clanking.

The scholars watched as townsmen were hunted down and dragged out into the open, their weapons taken, and their hands bound behind their backs. Not many fought against the soldiers.

The scholars began to dismantle the barricade at the hall doors.

"Now to find Giles," John said. "We must go to the fair, first."

Sebastian shook his head. "He would have fled for refuge at the first noise of trouble. We must check the halls and ask if any have seen him."

"Truth."

High Street was littered with the rent and charred fabric of tapestries. The cold February wind carried an occasional page, torn from a book and burnt on the edges, twisting and flapping as it sailed away. A bonfire made of stools, books, and other furniture still smoked in Carfax, the town square.

The horses had been let out of the stables on Horsemonger Street. Some of the buildings stood open and gutted by fire. Scholars went pelting by, looking for their belongings or their friends.

John and Sebastian searched out the halls until almost evening. At last Sebastian said, "Come, there's no putting it off, John. I've heard that many bodies were tossed into the Thames last night. We must ask for him there, at the river."

"At least if he's not among the dead, we can have good hope that he is alive and in hiding," John said.

"To the gates, then."

It was strange to see the stern soldiers at nearly every turn in Oxford. The houses were shuttered, and there was the sound of women weeping.

"I wonder how many they will arrest," Sebastian said.

"Or how many they have hanged," John added.

They went out the gates and walked along the wall until Sebastian pointed to a bonfire ahead where several of the footmen were gathered. The river passed close there, its grassy banks coming right up to the thoroughfare. There were men in Oxford robes lying on the grass, rows of them.

The despair and conviction of sin that had earlier seized my father made him stop. "I shall be sick," he said as a cart loaded with more bodies came up from the road downriver and pulled to a stop by the bonfire. It creaked down past the assortment of bodies and stopped. Two men jumped off to unload the new corpses. "I cannot look, John."

"Come, friend, we have seen much worse than this."

"Nay, John, I cannot. No more. Not innocents unarmed. My feet and stomach are all lead. I cannot."

John softened. "Very well, then. Stay here. I will go ahead and look for him."

"Forgive me, John."

"I do. You've risked much that would have caused many a brave man to faint—long before this."

John walked alone toward the fire. The chief of the guards bade him look.

As he himself told me in describing the scene, there seemed to be at least two dozen bodies there, but he knew Giles the moment that he saw him. The eyes were closed, and the lined face was drawn as though he had been concentrating on some disputation. His clothes were rent where he had been stabbed.

"Giles! And you so gentle and good!" John cried, dropping to his knees. "Who has done this? Who has killed you?"

Sebastian came running at the cry.

"Alas!" he exclaimed and dropped by John. "I knew it! I knew it when we saw the river! I knew we should find him here!" The big man's eyes filled with tears, and he took Giles by the shoulders. "What pleasure did they get in your death? And what had you done to merit their steel? I know it from looking at you! Nothing! Innocent as a lamb in spring!" He broke down with his face in his hands. "Why has God done this to us? Does He love to see us weep? It is as though He drinks the tears of men—we weep and never stop."

"Nay, Sebastian." John stopped his weeping and caught Sebastian by his shoulders. "Nay, do not blaspheme. It is Christ who weeps, not men. Do you think that all this came with His blessing? He has wept sore over Oxford's sins and over the sins of all England. Giles is with Christ, where none can strike him now."

Sebastian looked abashed. "God forgive me for my thoughts, John—I, who have received such mercy. It is as you say." He swallowed back his tears. "But it is a sore blow and such torment to think of the pain in which he died."

"He is free from pain, now. Thoughts of it torment us, but never him." Yet tears spilled out of John's eyes as he spoke. "I hear the horn. We must be inside before the gates close."

Both stood up and looked sorrowfully down on their slain companion.

"Come," said Sebastian, "before the gates close, and I will buy us a candle, John. We must talk this night, and I would see your face."

Candles were expensive, but Sebastian managed to shout his way into one of the closed shops in town and purchase one. They went to his room.

The town lay deathly silent, and the university seemed deserted. Sebastian lit the candle from the fire in the grate and stuck it upright on a piece of plank he had brought up. He sat on the floor, and John sat on the mattress.

In the wavering yellow light, the two scholars looked at each other.

"The university will be closed again," Sebastian said.

"Aye."

"What will you do?" the archer asked.

"Visit my brother in Yorkshire, I suppose, and pay my respects to John of Clairvaux, my old teacher who taught me Latin," John said. "And you?"

"Ah, you know the answer to that, John," Sebastian told him. "I shall go to my father, now that I must. And he shall hear every woe I have to tell him, and I shall remind him that I am his heir and the last to carry on the family name. And then we shall shoot at the mark morning by morning as I ply him to tell me stories of France and the battles. By my ten skilled fingers! He shall beg me to be a soldier before I'm done with him!"

"It sounds a good strategy," John admitted.

"And then, John, I shall marry the first fair lass I see and have my family. And I shall seek to forget the pains I have suffered this day and the loss of our gentle Giles. Now come and tell me I'm a rogue to leave Oxford and the priesthood!"

"Nay, I care not a straw for that," John said. "Better to marry and be a godfearing yeoman, I say. The priesthood imparts no special favor to a man."

"Ye think not? In truth, there's many a priest who ought to be run through, as we both well know. Still, the Church says—"

"Sebastian," John interrupted him, "let not the Church come between you and Christ. You would make an unhappy and sullen priest, and it would serve no purpose." John shook his head and added, "I say again, let not the Church come between you and Christ."

"What will I do without you to guide me to Him?" Sebastian asked.

"Nay, friend," John said. "Let not even John Wycliffe come between you and Christ. Christ is His own best teacher. A man's way to Him lies in the Holy Scripture. Think about St. John's Gospel, chapter one: *"In principio erat Verbum, et Verbum erat apud Deum, et Deus erat Verbum."* (In the beginning was the Word, and the Word was in the presence of God, and the Word was God.) If a man seeks to know the Scripture, that man seeks to know Christ. Abide by that, Sebastian, and cling to the Scripture regardless of what men say."

"I will, John. I will take the Scriptures with me," Sebastian told him. "And I promise you that I will read them. But you may have my other books, what few there are."

"I thank you."

"Take the mattress this last time. Tomorrow we may start out together, at least as far as Leicester, where I shall leave you."

"As you say. And we may talk then of Giles and perhaps be comforted. Good night."

"Good night, friend John." Sebastian blew out the candle, and it was dark.

PART TWO

Chapter Fourteen
Oxford Again
August, 1376

One and twenty years had passed since John Wycliffe blessed Sebastian Ayleton on the Leicester Road and bade him good-by through tears. And Sebastian Ayleton, from thence a changed man, went only briefly to France as an archer before he returned to his native soil and hung up his bow forever.

Five years after the fighting at Oxford, he married a "stout fair maid" of Leicester and settled down to managing his father's farm. But the only child to stand at his knee was I, for in the second year of his marriage the Pestilence returned to England, taking my sweet mother—his wife—and my younger brother, who was but an infant at the time.

Yet my father, Sebastian Ayleton, loved me enough for both mother and father. He it was who taught me my first Latin, and he it was who would often bid me—on a winter night when work was scarce and dark had not yet come—to take down his old Bible and read out a passage and translate it for him.

When the time came, he hired a tutor to continue me in my studies, and he began to talk of sending me to Oxford.

Oxford for me was no grim-sounding name. Nay, the stories of Fleet Nigel and Giles and John of Wycliffe had been my meat and drink. Rather than war stories, Father told me Oxford stories, and these excited my imagination much more than details of the battle at Calais or those other foreign-sounding places.

Others would talk of Edward the Black Prince, Charles of Navarre, and Sir John Hawkwood, but I longed to hear of the meals at the Kicking Pony, the death of Giles, the sights of the fair. These were the stories, when I was a lad, that brought the laughter to my lips or the tears to my eyes.

My father had kept up with news of John Wycliffe and had translated it to fit my boyish mind. I knew that John Wycliffe was finally a doctor at Oxford, that his lectures drew large crowds of the students, that he had served briefly as a King's chaplain, and that he had addressed Parliament on the matter of paying taxes to the pope.

My father had seen the pope's splendid castle at Avignon, in France, and he had learned of how the pope was not above hiring private soldiers or even assassins to carry out his will: to impose papal taxes, to curb unruly nobles, to bring cardinals or archbishops into line, or—if necessary—to kill them and appoint others in their place.

Thus, when Pope Urban V demanded that England pay him tribute money, my father's anger rose.

"Are we each and every man a slave to a Roman that sits in France?" he had roared. "Is England nothing and King Edward nothing, that the pope would claim us as vassals? Is this the man who claims to represent Christ?"

There were many others of my father's mind, for—as you realize—in laying claim to tribute from the King, the pope was claiming to be the rightful ruler of England. He was pretending that King Edward held power only by papal authority. Father rejoiced when he heard that John Wycliffe had been summoned to Parliament to give his views on the tribute money. I, being too young at the time to understand fully, was nonetheless persuaded that some great good had happened and that John Wycliffe would take care of us all.

And he did, too. He convinced Parliament from Scripture that spiritual authority should be always separate from political authority, ever since the time of our Lord.

It was a treatise—I suppose—that the pope did not care for, nor did any of those abbots, bishops, and archbishops who were turning a pretty penny by ruling the lives of the peasants around them. But King Edward was behind John Wycliffe, and the Church could not harm him.

When I was older and able to understand, I learned from my father that the Doctor was teaching clearly what had been in the heart of many a learned Englishman: the Church had too much money and too much power; its officials were corrupt, and many of its doctrines contained serious error. Wycliffe's bold preaching at last was making him a public enemy to the Church.

"The Church will bide its time, William," my father told me, "like the great, preying beast that it is, but it will seek, nonetheless, to destroy him. Pray God that the King stays hale and hardy and able to keep out those interfering Dominicans and their infernal Inquisition."

I promised I would. And soon, my tutor claimed me to be as ready in Latin as Augustine himself. My father had heard that the Reverend Doctor Wycliffe had undertaken a new project, and thus he bade me go help him until the autumn term started, to serve as best as I could through all my stay at Oxford, and to make myself dear to him.

So commanding, he gave me a purse of silver, a stout staff, and his blessing. And thus, at sixteen, in August of the final year of Edward's reign, I at last set out for Oxford and the profound doctor, John Wycliffe.

Chapter Fifteen
John Wycliffe's Translation

The town of Oxford was much bigger than any hamlet in Leicester. I asked my way to Queen's College, where I told the regent-master that I had come with a letter to present to the Reverend Doctor John Wycliffe. With a squint at my rustic clothes, he told me the way to the Doctor's rooms.

He had been more polite to have taken me himself, but I said nothing and found the way. The autumn term was still two months off, and Queen's was quiet.

As I approached the door to which I had been directed, I feared that I would find the room empty. Dr. Wycliffe had a church in Lutterworth, usually run by a curate, yet he often would retire there to preach himself. Perhaps he had gone there for the summer.

I knocked on the great solid door, and there was instantly a clattering in the room and a man's voice saying, "I could have answered to it, Nicholas!"

And the door was swung open by a man scarce ten years older than myself.

"If you please, I have come to present a letter to the Reverend Doctor Wycliffe. My name is William Ayleton," I said.

From inside, the same voice said, "Hark! Ayleton did he say? Bid him enter! Why, could it be?"

And before I could walk in, there appeared an older man with a white beard and white hair, clad in a russet brown robe, with nothing on his feet. He looked slender as a birch twig, but the hand that grasped mine and pulled me inside was as strong as many a man's.

"It is! I know the curly hair and brown eyes, round as coins! Art thy father's son!" And he embraced me.

To speak truly, I had heard so much of the thunderings of this prophet, that—despite my father's descriptions to the contrary—I had imagined John Wycliffe to be a giant of a man, with a great chest and broad shoulders and curling grey hair.

Yet here was one who looked frail and sickly and old. I was, for a moment, disappointed in him, but the embrace was so welcome (I was already homesick), his joy at the sight of me so sincere, his kindness so evident, that before he had let me go I had come to love him.

"Boys!" he exclaimed to the other two who were in the room. "This is one dearly beloved—William, son of Sebastian Ayleton, a lad I came with to Oxford. Clear the table of papers, now, and let us set out the little that we have." He looked at me. "You are hungry and weary, no doubt, my son. You'll spend the night, of course." He had the letter from my father in his hand, but he clasped me again and asked, "What business brings you to Oxford in August? Nothing ill has befallen your father, I trust?"

"Nay, Doctor. My father has sent me to you. 'Tis all in the letter you hold."

"Ah." He looked a bit puzzled but immediately sat down at the table and opened the letter. I took the opportunity to glance at the room. There was a grate with a low fire in it, the table that had been covered with books, a few shelves on the wall, and a second door that led to another small room.

At his invitation I sat by him while the other two set out bread, honey, and cheese. One of them disappeared out the door and soon came back with a pitcher and some cups.

They both were Masters or Bachelors of Theology. That much I could judge by their gowns and hoods. And they seemed a little curious about me but friendly enough, ready to accept me at their master's bidding. Wycliffe later introduced them as Nicholas Hereford and John Purvey. Of their own consent they were assisting him at his work.

"Ah, Sebastian's hand grows cramped," the aged Doctor said. "It is hard for me to spell out the words. Read it, if you will, my son."

I complied:

To my dear friend and master John Wycliffe, Reverend Doctor and evangelist of God:
I send unto you my son William Ayleton, trained from his birth to fear God, to love learning, and to have a regard for the Holy Scriptures. He is well taught and a bright lad, and he is ready to begin at Oxford. I have sent him to you now, what with some who assist you having departed, that he might play a part as a servant of God in translating the Scriptures.

Your Servant,
Sebastian Ayleton

I pray you, if he fail you in any way, to tenderly regard him as one beloved of his father, your dear friend.

I was, of course, blushing as I finished reading this to him, but the beloved Doctor smiled on me as I set the paper down.

"You shall not fail me, my son. I have no fear of that at all." He took the letter from me and put it into a pocket of his robe. Then he glanced at Hereford and Purvey. "An assistant. We have need of another," he said.

However, the two younger men looked sore distressed and perplexed.

"Master," Hereford said after an awkward pause, "do you think that a grammar school lad can undertake this task?"

I looked at Wycliffe. "I beg pardon, sir, but do I understand that you are translating the Scriptures?"

"Aye, my son. Your father has long known and assisted me in it with his money."

So that was the rub. Father had been generous to them, and they thought it unthankful to refuse me a place in this task, though they doubted my skill.

I glanced at the man named Nicholas Hereford. "Master," I said, "I know I seem a stripling to a man of your attainments, and in truth, if we undertook a disputation, you would soon have the best of me. Yet my training in Latin came from no mere grammar school. Set any passage of Jerome's Vulgate before me, and you will find me competent."

"Competency is admirable, my lad," Hereford said. "But we must have expertise."

"Do as he asks you, Nicholas," said Wycliffe. "It is only fair. Bring the book of Isaiah to me, and I will select a passage."

Hereford obeyed. The Doctor scanned through the pages and at last said, "I shall read it to you, my son, and you shall tell me what I have spoken:

Quam pulchri super montes pedes adnuntiantis et
praedicantis pacem
adnuntiantis bonum praedicantis salutem
dicentis Sion regnavit Deus tuus.

And when he had finished, I said it back to him in English, answering thus with my translation:

"How beautiful upon the mountains are the feet of the one announcing and of the one preaching peace;
of the one announcing good; of the one preaching salvation;
of the one saying, 'Your God reigns in Zion.'"

Wycliffe slapped his hand upon the table. "Excellent! He speaks as a master!"

"I confess he has a fair grasp of Latin," Hereford admitted. "Yet it does take more than that—"

"Aye, I know." Wycliffe waved it away. "He shall not translate, son Nicholas. He shall proofread. There, what say you to that?"

"I could choose no better man," Hereford agreed, and his comrade Purvey nodded.

"Good, now let us eat and be merry. My enemies call me a glutton, son William, yet I apologize for this bare board. I promise, you shall visit the Kicking Pony with me and taste of their savory meat pies." So saying, he served us as cordially as though he were the Duke himself.

In truth, I had heard of the beloved Doctor being called a glutton by his foes, and it was a marvel to see him eat. He was well mannered and cheerful, yet he could stow away food like a sailor.

"It is my failing," he told me when he saw my eyes get big as he cut himself more cheese. "I overeat, and I am always hungry, yet for the life of me I know not where the food goes, for I'm slighter now than when your father knew me."

"Eating from hunger is no sin, dear father," Purvey said gently. "The popes and cardinals eat when they are full and load their tables with many dainties. Thus they easily accuse others of the sins that they themselves fall into."

"Possibly, possibly," the Doctor said. He looked at me with his bright eye. "But come, tell me of your father, lad. You are the apple of his eye, and it must be hard for both of you to be apart. Sebastian Ayleton is my senior by three years. Yet his hair is still brown and his arm strong, eh?"

"Yes. He enjoys excellent health, Doctor. And I do miss him."

"And he you, I'm sure. I recall him, not long after we met, trying to get directions with me at Carfax. And what did he do but seize a Dominican and crack him on his pate? I felt pressed to reprove him, yet it was so funny—the

Dominican with his welt and Sebastian gripping his long bow."

Hereford and Purvey smiled politely, but it was meat and drink to me to hear the familiar stories. The Doctor reminisced about the disputations, about his early studies, and the very first spiritual truths that had laid hold of him. The other two became interested, and we sat 'round the table until the only light came from the embers in the grate.

The two assistants at last groped their way to the door and bade us good night, and the Doctor took me into the other room, where he bid me take his bed, which was a mattress on the floor.

I protested, and I think that when he saw how distressed I was to think of his sleeping on the floor, he took his own bed. I took the blanket and slept before the fire.

Chapter Sixteen
A Summons from the Duke

It not being my intention to take holy orders, I did not enter a hall, nor did I submit to being made a subdeacon. I instead found a good hostelry, with a room to myself, and spent my days proofreading Wycliffe's English Bible.

It was a project not yet well known at Oxford, though from the way Nicholas Hereford talked and boasted about it, I suspected everybody would know about it once the term began.

Hereford was a kind man, but very talkative and excitable. He was preparing for his doctorate and was very much interested in Wycliffe's treatises and lectures. Purvey, somewhat calmer by nature yet still quite zealous, was Wycliffe's secretary. He was also a scholar and was much taken up with the teachings of Wycliffe.

"God gives light and understanding to His chosen warriors, my lad," Purvey once said to me. "And thus He has given to our beloved doctor. He sees to the papacy and through the papacy. And if he has his way, the English Church shall be rent from that corpulent beast. Then perhaps we may return to the purity and holiness of the Church as Christ ordained it, with no mere man presuming to be the vicar of Christ!"

That title, "the vicar of Christ," had been introduced years ago, long before my birth, by Pope Innocent. It means— for those who read no Latin—that the pope stands in the place of Christ on earth, having His full authority. The Doctor had told us that much protest had greeted Innocent's claim, and some of the Church leaders in that day had recognized it as blasphemy, but nothing availed against it. The pope retained the title.

I could understand Hereford's and Purvey's antagonism against the pope. I felt it myself. Many a free Englishman felt it. But, as I proofread the Scripture for them, and heard their talk, I began to see what seemed to be a contradiction in their thinking.

First I must explain what the Scripture at last did to me. The plain, pure Scripture, freed from its many interpretations—called *glosses* by the scholars—came to be both delight and enigma to me. It held promise; it held delight; it held terror. Of course most of the people at Oxford studied the glosses much more than they did the actual verses. Thus they were more caught up in interpreting the interpretations than in the actual message from God's Word.

It was the Scripture—as I thoughtfully read it in that room—that converted me. I came to know, as the book of Jonah said: *"Salvation is of the Lord."* Not of man's merit, but by the blood of Christ, which no man and no church can apply but Christ only. And thus I cried to Christ for salvation, and even as I did, His blessed Spirit comforted mine, and I knew that He forgave me by His grace.

Eventually I had a dilemma in listening to Hereford and Purvey. For with them, it was "Wycliffe says this!" and "Wycliffe says that!" They were often comparing their notes on what the Doctor said. It was not my place to say anything, for I was the youngest in the room, not yet a student, and only the proofreader. But I wondered if Hereford and Purvey might not be in danger of falling into the same trap that had caught so many others: weighing the words of a man over the words of the Bible.

Not that I questioned their conversions. They lived godly lives, certainly enough. And they did love the Scripture. But I saw that they did look much to John Wycliffe and relied upon him to explain Scripture to them—hardly the attitude one would expect in the disciples of a man who said *Scripture only!*

The Doctor, always eager to discuss Scripture and his findings, did not pay much regard to how much they relied on him. He was—after all—a lecturer, and he expected his students to ask him questions. And soon I had other concerns as well and did not think much more of the loyalties of Hereford and Purvey.

There came a day in mid-September when a fellow came knocking in the early morning to tell me he was bound for Leicester and would deliver a packet to my father if I so wished. For him, of course, it was a handy way to get sixpence. I longed to write to my father, so I bade the fellow meet me at the Kicking Pony in an hour.

I hurried to purchase ink and paper, and I wrote out a letter to my father telling him of all that had passed since my arrival. It took more nearly two hours than one; so I hastened to the Kicking Pony.

The fellow was there, much put out by my tardiness; so I purchased him his breakfast and mine, delivered him the letter, and paid him.

By then, morning mass was long past, and I hurried to Queen's Hall, expecting Hereford and Purvey to be put out with me, as the messenger had been.

Yet when I entered the room, they were all intent on something else. Even the Doctor was there, which was unusual in the mornings. He had a paper in his hand.

"My masters," I said, "I beg pardon. Is something amiss?"

Wycliffe looked at me. "Naught amiss, my son. Only a shock. The Duke of Lancaster, third son of the King, has summoned me to London."

Chapter Seventeen
Preaching in London

There is no need to pretend that John of Gaunt, then Duke of Lancaster, shared our beliefs. He only half understood them, and even then only from the political viewpoint.

I suppose the Duke was a religious man, and I have heard from learned men that he was a man of honor. But the Duke was an aristocrat, one of the nobility, and I think that there lies the heart of his friendship with our beloved Doctor.

That same year, many of the landowning common people elected or appointed several men to represent them to Parliament in London. Much to the surprise of the Duke of Lancaster, Parliament did give this group of "commons" a few rights. This group, which in my lifetime came to be called the House of Commons, had demanded the arrests of two of the nobility. They had also demanded the banishment of one Alice Perrers, a favorite of the King at Court and a ruthless, brilliant, and dangerous woman.

The Duke of Lancaster, presiding over Parliament, had opposed the commons. He thought they were nothing but a bunch of meddlers who had no business interfering with the nobility. And he thought that Parliament had no business granting anything to the commons.

Parliament took offense. And many bishops and archbishops were members of Parliament, and they took offense, too. Thus it fell, with the Duke of Lancaster opposing the church officials and they opposing him. And in this case, the favor of the common people was with the bishops, because the people wanted a say in government. The Duke of Lancaster had to find a way to turn the people against the church officials.

To sum up, the Duke of Lancaster unleashed John Wycliffe on the London churches to preach. To preach whatever he saw fit to preach, which of course was on the need for the English Church to be free of papal control, to return to the Scripture, and to throw off the gross corruptions of the wealthy clergy.

The Londoners welcomed him. He was convincing; he was right; and he lived in holy poverty, unlike the wealthy abbots, friars, and bishops. When John Wycliffe urged the clergy to give up wealth and power as Christ did upon earth, he was asking them to do no more than he himself had done. He had no wealth, no position, nothing but his russet brown robe, the garment of a serf.

Meanwhile, lectures had begun at Oxford. I learned the disputation and the science of rhetoric and logic. But I was marked at Oxford as one of the Wycliffites, and it was difficult to make friends more suited to my age than Hereford and Purvey. All wanted to hear what I said of this or that, and few there were who wanted to know William Ayleton. I also began to understand the trials of John Wycliffe, for if I ate twice a week at an inn, I was a glutton and unfit for Wycliffe. But if I did without and stayed at my studies, I was a brash young man trying to ape my superiors.

Despite these conflicts, ever in my heart I was waiting for the return of the beloved Doctor. My father bade me serve him and be dear to him; yet it was he who had served me and was dear to me.

Hereford and Purvey sometimes received word of him. They were quite busy giving lectures themselves, as well as attending them. The work on the translation slowed considerably, though it never quite stopped.

"He is well. He is well," Hereford would assure me whenever we saw each other and I invariably asked after Wycliffe. "Lad, think you that the clergy dare harm him? He is under the protection of Christ. None shall touch him."

"Master," I retorted, somewhat hot with impatience, "our souls be safe with Christ, but the true Church has ever had her martyrs. Think you that the Bishop of London will meekly sit by while the Doctor castigates the clergy and the people cheer him on?"

"Bishop Courtenay dares not harm him, William. Besides, the Bishop is a learned and temperate man. He may profit by the Doctor's preaching." With that or some other equally naive remark, Hereford would hurry off to his next lecture.

Many a time I contained my exasperation and muttered, "Hereford, you dreamer!" after him. He could not see that the lines of this battle were drawn. And I was sure, once the Bishop or the Archbishop made up their minds, that they would seek to silence John Wycliffe.

November and December passed, and the New Year was rung in with all well. And then, two days after the Feast of St. Scholastica, one of the Duke's men brought us word that the Archbishop of Canterbury, Simon Sudbury, and the Bishop of London, William Courtenay, had summoned the Doctor to St. Paul's to be examined on his beliefs. He had one week to prepare his defenses.

It was a trial. And his judges would be those same men whom he had denounced. Any man familiar with the politics of the Church knew very well what could happen: treachery. Wycliffe could very likely be imprisoned, perhaps killed, or at least defrocked and shamed and banished from Oxford.

"Let us go," Hereford said to Purvey. "We shall die with him."

"I shall go too," I said.

Both men looked at me. I could sense that they thought this no time for a newcomer to follow along, and so I left them to themselves. Alone, I ran down Horsemonger Street, borrowed a horse and trappings, and galloped toward the city gates and London.

On the way out of Oxford I passed Nicholas and John and cried, "I shall await you there!" Hereford looked a little confused, but Purvey waved.

I had the audacity to go to the Savoy Palace, the Duke's London residence, and take a message to the porter for John Wycliffe from one of his students. The porter bid me wait in the yard, and so I dismounted. Not long after, the Doctor himself came racing across the flagstones.

He grasped me in his embrace, and I—fearing for his life—clung to him a moment.

"You have as fiery and true a spirit as your father!" he cried. He stepped back and looked at me. "The porter would have brought you up, but I couldn't wait. But come now, and be refreshed."

"Pardon me," I begged. "I am not ready for the Duke's palace, being dusty and ill dressed. I only sought to see how it fares with you, Doctor."

He looked on me gently. "Do you fear for me? This is no Inquisition, my son, but a convocation of clergy. A fair trial of English clergymen. I could ask no more than that they should hear me."

"Dear Doctor, it would not be wise to pretend they do not hate you," I told him. "They do not seek to listen, only to entrap you."

He smiled a faint smile, as though rueful, perhaps, to hear fears which he himself had just quenched.

"Look," he said, glancing around at the gray stone walls of the Savoy courtyard. "It is the work of men, William, and none stronger, though quite ugly. Yet it shall not last. The work of God, now, is lovely for those who can see it, and He does not guard it by man's strength but by His own. God's work shall last forever." He looked at me again. "If

John Wycliffe belongs to God, he cannot be destroyed, nor can men even touch his body unless God so wills. Fear not. This is not for my death, my son, but to prove those who will follow Christ."

He seemed serene, and I could not help but sense the irony—he so slight and old and calm, and I so big and strong and afraid.

As though he read my thought, he said, "How like your father you look. And he also, when set upon by forces too great for him, became a tempered man. You shall profit by this."

I bowed my head and after a moment mounted my horse. But I leaned down to grasp his hand in farewell. "Send me word of where you stay in London," he said. "I shall see you if I can."

I nodded, too full to speak words, and left him.

Chapter Eighteen
The London Riot
February, 1377

My country eyes had never seen the likes of London. In the chill dawn light, professional water carriers jostled with housewives in the narrow streets, bringing their water crocks, buckets, and jars up from the conduits. Hens, geese, and pigs ran across the cobbles, heedless of the people, seeking scraps of food from the trash that lay everywhere.

Ragged men groped for alms or skulked along the sides of the buildings. Better-dressed men with short tunics and tight leggings lounged in front of taverns and in other doorways. Women, some arrayed in simple dresses and some quite brazenly dressed, hurried along the streets or strolled at their ease.

And above all rose the clucking and clamour and rattling and banging that was London. I wish never to go there again, but I put a brave face on it during my stay and managed to get a room for myself without being bilked, rifled, or murdered in my sleep. When I did not think of the beloved Doctor, I found myself thinking of my father. For though I was, like him, a great strapping lad, he had more raw courage than I, and he would have turned a jolly eye on the crowded, inhospitable city and made me merry.

I was somewhat miserable during my stay. For one thing— as I had already guessed—the Duke was not letting Wycliffe out of his sight until the convocation convened. For another, the few Londoners I talked to were incensed against the Duke of Lancaster. No one would listen to my tale of woe for Wycliffe, because as soon as I mentioned the Duke, every Londoner within earshot would jump to his feet growling.

And, yes, I knew why. The Duke of Lancaster was seeking to amass power behind the crown. The king was old and inept, and Edward the Black Prince, was dead. His son Richard, heir to the throne, was but a lad—not yet twelve years old. It was the Duke of Lancaster who had a hand on the reins of the kingdom. He was drawing the cords of power tighter. And though I thought it good for him to take power from the Church, the Londoners were fiercely angry with him. He had offended William Courtenay, the Bishop of London, and he had made a motion in Parliament to deprive London of its mayor and keep the city under the control of the crown.

To me, country lad that I was, this news was only a heap of eggs in moonshine. What cared I who governed London? But the Londoners were furious. For they had a charter, and they had certain rights, and all would be made void if they came under direct control of the crown. And William Courtenay, their bishop, was on their side in this. The Duke of Lancaster had not backed Courtenay down, not an inch.

After a few days in London I was joined by Hereford and Purvey. Hereford seemed a bit put out by my resolute manner in seeking out Wycliffe and entrenching myself in London.

"You're an impulsive boy," he remarked to me after I had made them welcome in my small room in a hostelry near St. Paul's Cathedral. "You've missed almost a week of lectures, and for what purpose?"

"To play the snoop in London," I told him.

"And what have you found?" he demanded.

"Only that the people support the Bishop against the Duke, and no one seems to realize that the Bishop may very well imprison our Doctor."

Purvey put a hand on my shoulder. "Impulsive, yes," he told me, and he smiled at Master Nicholas, "but no more impulsive than another I could name, who also would have sped to London had he but a horse. Fear not, young William. Courtenay shall not lay hands on the Doctor. Know you not that Wycliffe is under the Duke of Lancaster's protection?"

"What can the Duke do when the people hate him so?" I asked.

"For himself, not much, though they dare not touch him. But do you think that Courtenay will risk losing their favor by bringing Wycliffe to harm? I say nay, not unless he has the pope behind him. And—as yet—he does not. The pope dare not move while King Edward lives and the Duke of Lancaster is wielding power."

"The pope shall never strike at Wycliffe," Hereford said. "He would not dare."

I glanced in surprise at Master Hereford. I thought it very likely that the pope would dare. But Purvey answered nothing, and presently our talk turned to more immediate concerns, such as where and when the convocation would be held.

St. Paul's was not really one building but many, including the bishop's palace. The cathedral itself had a spire that one could see from almost anywhere in London, and inside, the nave was longer and much wider than any street in England. Lawyers and clerks and their clients met and conferred at St. Paul's. Books were sold there, and I had heard that on most days it had the air of a busy, thronging place, perhaps a little like a fair.

On the morning of February nineteenth, we three set out long before morning mass was said, yet even so there were already people flocking toward the cathedral, more bent, I thought, on witnessing this clash between Bishop and Duke than on weighing out the truths in the sermons preached by Wycliffe.

Yet we were early enough to push our way through the cathedral to the east end, where we had to wait for mass to be finished before we could enter the Chapel of the Blessed Virgin. This was the assigned chapel where the convocation of prelates would examine our beloved Doctor.

"In truth," Hereford observed as more and more people came crowding in, "if this mass of people becomes a mob, we shall be crushed."

"We came to die with him, did we not?" I asked.

Purvey stifled a smile and put his hand on my shoulder. "Be not so satiric, lad. Nor so on edge. The Doctor is yet as safe as he ever was, as are we."

Hereford took the jab well. "It would be a waste for him to be crushed before he ever set foot in the chapel. I hope he will walk in ahead of the Duke, that we might all be together when they rush Lancaster."

Purvey looked serious. "Truth, it does smell like a fight."

"Yes, that and tripe and onions," Hereford added.

I relaxed and laughed at his joke. Thereafter we waited in amiable silence.

More and more people crowded inside, and I could tell from the huge din of voices that not only the large Chapel of the Blessed Virgin but also the nave of the cathedral was crammed full. The noise was deafening. All the talk was of the Duke, and the imprisonment of Peter de la Mare, another favorite of the people.

As the gorgeous procession of bishops entered to take their seats, a wave of silence suddenly swept over us from end to end, even out into the cathedral. It is quite an impressive thing when ten or twelve thousand men instantly hush.

All mitred and vestured, Archbishop Sudbury led the way. He was a mild-looking man, impressive by his clothing and attendants, but not imposing by his face. By contrast, the Bishop of London, William Courtenay, who came immediately after the archbishops and led the bishops, was young, stern, and regal. He carried himself as a commander or prince, and when he took his seat alongside Sudbury, it was with one hand on his staff and one on his thigh, his knees spread as though a sword lay across them. Bishop Courtenay had come to judge, fully believing in his own right and authority.

Wycliffe is doomed, I thought. For I knew that the Bishop would not budge, and I also knew that the beloved Doctor would not budge.

But just then we heard the noise of a great commotion. From the back of the chapel there was a tumult of noise: jeering and hissing and gruff commands.

There then came up among the people several men-at-arms wearing the uniform of the Duke of Lancaster's service—three lions passant. These men were making way for four friars—all doctors from Oxford—and behind them John Wycliffe, looking small and frail but composed. Last of all came the Duke himself and Sir Henry Percy, who had recently become the Marshal of England, and who was now waiting to assume power in London. These two were ringed by both the Duke's men and Percy's men. And it was well that they were, for the people—not much heeding Wycliffe—looked ready to tear them apart.

Archbishop Sudbury seemed quite at a loss, but the Bishop raised his hand, and so commanding was he that all fell silent again.

"Lord Percy, if I had known what show of force you would have brought into the church, I would have stopped you coming thither," Bishop Courtenay said.

We had been pushing to get closer to the Duke's party, and I saw the flush on Lord Percy's cheek at being rebuked. But he had no answer.

The Duke spoke up. "He may keep such show of force here, though you say so."

Percy, relieved at being defended, turned to Wycliffe and gestured to one of the few empty chairs. "Wycliffe, sit down," he said. "For you have many things to answer to, and you need to repose yourself on a soft seat."

Bishop Courtenay, without seeming offended, waved a hand to check the polite invitation. "It is unreasonable that one cited before Church judgment should sit during his answer. He must and shall stand."

"We have regard for the Bishop's authority," Percy rejoined. "Has the Bishop no regard for age? The Reverend Doctor shall sit, at my invitation."

"The Lord Percy's motion is but reasonable," the Duke of Lancaster shouted. "As for you, my Lord Bishop, who are grown so proud and arrogant, I will bring down the pride, not of you alone but of all the prelates in England!"

The Duke's boast was not well received. The crowd around him gathered closer, scowling, and there were some rough answers thrown down, which he ignored.

"Do your worst, sir," Courtenay told him.

"Ho, you bear yourself proudly for your parents' sake, who shall not be able to help you," the Duke of Lancaster retorted. "They shall have enough to do to help themselves!"

At this threat, which even to me seemed bullying and crude—to threaten the Bishop's family—another tremor of anger at the Duke of Lancaster ran through the crowd.

"My confidence is not in my parents nor in any man else, but only in God, in whom I trust, by whose assistance I will be bold to speak!" Courtenay exclaimed.

It was well answered, and I do freely confess that any human heart would have despised the bullying of the Duke of Lancaster and warmed to the courage of the Bishop, though the Bishop meant ill to the cause of Christ. Several cried out in approval of his brave words.

The Duke flushed at the Bishop's contempt of him and the crowd's approval of the Bishop. "Rather than take these words at his hands," he cried to Lord Percy, "I would drag the Bishop by the hair out of the church!" And he clapped his hands to his belt as though ready to stride up and do it.

I took the Duke of Lancaster for a man of many hot words, so I did not suppose he would carry out any one of his many threats. But at his statement, several of the

townsmen burst forth on him, crying, "Sacrilege! He would lay hands on the Bishop!"

The cry of "sacrilege" rang through the nave, and instantly the men-at-arms tried to push the people back from the Duke and Sir Percy.

By then the cry had gone to the nave of St. Paul's, and those nearest us were screaming, "Thrust him out! Thrust him out!"

The Bishop cried out for them to desist and be silent in the house of God, but by then the whole of St. Paul's was in a tumult, what with the violent cries of "sacrilege" and two-thirds of the people not being able to see what had happened. And meanwhile, the Duke of Lancaster roared at everybody, and his men-at-arms were also shouting at the people and cursing them for rebels and insolent dogs, and then the crowd began to surge, like the tide upon the beach. We were moved back and forth with them as many pressed toward the Duke.

Archbishop Sudbury glanced at Bishop Courtenay as though seeking counsel, and Courtenay, with an expression of displeasure and chagrin, threw down his hand and then waved it at the Duke and Wycliffe, dismissing them. The men-at-arms kept their weapons ready should any try violence, and thus the Duke of Lancaster and Henry Percy, with much struggle, passed through, but with the press all around them and crying against them. At any moment I expected the killing to start, but suddenly—as we also were swept with the crowd—I found myself but two arm lengths from Wycliffe.

He had been forgotten by the crowd and must have urged those guarding him to guard the Duke. Now he was only trying to get out.

I struggled with my arms out as a man does who walks against a strong current of water, and at last I clapped his shoulder.

"William!" he cried. "So there you are! And Nicholas and John!"

"Stay with us—we shall be better off together," I begged him.

"Yes, yes. This has the feel of blood and fighting," he said. "Let us flee at once."

We pushed with the surge of people and got out at last. There was no fighting—at least not much—that day, but it hung in the air like a storm.

"God delivered me," the Doctor said firmly. "Let us make haste to Oxford."

We agreed and left that confused city that same day. And it was well, for the fighting erupted the next, and some were killed. Bishop Courtenay came out a great favorite over the Duke of Lancaster, for it was the Bishop who restored peace. London kept its mayor, and Oxford kept John Wycliffe.

Chapter Nineteen
A Rumor of Trouble

In June of that same year, King Edward III died, and the country mourned. He was a great king for England: valiant, merciful, and noble. No one had ever commanded him, but he had commanded all and in every circumstance. He had held back the pope's power in England, and he had crippled the Inquisition on our soil.

It was truly a time to wonder what would now become of us under Richard II, who was but a boy. Richard's mother, the fair Joan of Kent, still lived and seemed well favored toward our beloved Doctor. But Bishop Courtenay was our enemy in dead earnest, and I could fairly foretell that as our influence grew, so would his pent-up wrath.

In the summer months, many of Wycliffe's students and friends put on the plain robe and departed for the countryside to preach. They were called the "poor priests," though not every one of them was ordained by the Church.

Rather, they were ordained of God, and they went with their translations of the Gospels to read them to the people and to preach. And many a fat friar did they shame, for the friars would tell fables and old wives tales and Greek myths to the common folk and then call that preaching, that they might beg money.

I longed to go, too, and I would have, but the Doctor would not allow it.

"No. You are too young, lad. You must learn the Scripture better," he chided.

"I could read it to the people," I protested. "And what friar knows it as well as I?"

"Some do. You might yet run across one doughty friar who could fence you well with knowledge of theology."

Occasionally, Hereford or Purvey or one of the others would come and spend a day with the Doctor and tell all that had been done.

The peasants truly loved them, for our poor priests went out with no money; yet not one starved along the way. And when they read to the people at some well or crossroads or juncture of two fields, they would ask the listeners if any of them could read. Perhaps one man might step forward and have the Holy Gospel placed in his hands. Then he himself—for the first time in his life and in the history of all England—would read aloud God's Word in the common language. Many a man wept to do it, and I could well believe so, for they were learning that the Word of God Himself had come to be handled by men and touched by them.

In truth, the God of the Bible was quite different from what the abbots and bishops had been presenting to men.

It also fell at this time that many a parish priest came seeking to hear the Bible read. Some even came to the Doctor himself, asking his guidance.

He at once started a treatise and a collection of simple, straightforward sermons that priests could use.

And thus began my second year at Oxford.

I heard no lectures from Doctor Wycliffe, for he was called again to preach before Parliament about the matter of paying alms to the pope. This gave me hope that Wycliffe was yet strong enough to be safe from Bishop Courtenay.

I had spent a good part of the summer with Wycliffe, proofreading Hereford's translations that had been left for the summer. And now I began to miss the beloved Doctor. Hereford was back, and we two kept some company together, as he told me of the poor priests and all that had befallen them. But Purvey was with the Doctor at Westminster, and I found—even more so than during my first year—that I had few real friends. I had spent most of my time either at study or at proofreading, and the hostelry did not have the close companionship of any of the halls.

Indeed, my days at the hostelry were desolate, and if I went to an inn, even the Kicking Pony, there was none to share a meal with. October faded into a dismal November, gray and cheerless.

Then one day Nicholas Hereford came racing up to me on the street, his breath spouting in white plumes in the cool damp air.

"News!" he exclaimed, stopping me. "Have you heard the rumor of the pope's order?"

"No."

"It is said that the Holy Father will put Oxford under his control unless Wycliffe is put to the question and imprisoned!"

"Who told you so?" I asked.

"It is all over the University! A clerk at Parliament blurted it out!" he told me.

"Has no one received word from the pope?"

Hereford shrugged. "Who can say? If he sent word to the king, there may have been some confusion with the passing away of Edward and the ascension of Richard. The bulls may have been sent and then recalled. But the news has leaked out."

"It may be but a rumor," I told him.

"No, it was said before the whole Parliament, and Courtenay did not deny having knowledge of it."

"Who told you this?"

"Philip Repton. He spoke of it to Chancellor Tonworth, and the Chancellor had also heard about it."

Repton was one who had gone preaching in the countryside. He was a solid, quiet sort. If he had spread the word to Hereford, it was likely so.

"Has Wycliffe been arrested?" I asked him.

"Nay, the pope's order has not been received, but it is on the way."

"Will they let him come back to Oxford?"

"The prelates have no choice," Hereford said with an air of some importance. "The pope cannot move against an Englishman—especially an Oxford man—without the King's permission."

"When is he coming back, then?"

"I suppose it will be soon. They are finished with him."

As Hereford predicted, Wycliffe appeared again at his rooms by the first of December. I was pleased when Purvey came to get me at the hostelry. The Doctor had sent him.

Chapter Twenty
Another Urgent Message

The beloved Doctor greeted me with an embrace.

"How like your father you look—it is so remarkable!" he said.

"Doctor, what is this about the pope's order to imprison you?" I asked.

"Ah, all the tongues are wagging about me, I see," he said. "Well, it is so, my son. If I am found teaching what I do teach, then I am to be imprisoned and questioned, and you know all the rest of it. But I have received no official word. I hear that there are papal orders on the way."

He let me go and gestured that I sit at his table, where Purvey and some of the other translators were making ready to eat with him.

He took his seat and served us, as was his custom; yet not one of us could bear to eat. He merrily tucked into the herring and bread and after a few minutes glanced up at us.

"What makes you so solemn?" he asked.

"Is not this the arm of the Inquisition?" Purvey asked, speaking for all of us.

"No, it's a plate of herring," he returned. "Though we could have gotten us a joint of mutton."

"Doctor, you mock us!" I exclaimed.

"Ah, look at you—all so frightened! Did you think," he asked, "that we should preach the truth without the devil's onslaught? Did you think that corruption in the Church would roll over and make room for truth?"

None answered. He looked at each one of us in turn. Being ready to stand by him in trouble, I gladly met his eye, and so did one John Aston, but the others—even John Purvey—looked down.

"I see," he said after the long silence. "No, my dear sons. The two cannot lie side by side. We are locked in deadly combat, and in that combat, John Wycliffe may yield up his life. He may be killed, perhaps even by burning. But the truth shall exterminate the error in the end."

"Will not the Duke of Lancaster help you?" Purvey asked.

And I asked at the same time, "Oxford is under the King, isn't it? Doesn't that make you safe?"

Suddenly there was a babble of questions as we all spoke at once, suggesting ways for him to be safe. He raised his hand, and after a few seconds silence fell.

"Oxford may do as it pleases," he said. "The Duke may do as he pleases, and the pope may do as he pleases. John Wycliffe shall do as God pleases, and the first—and most sensible—matter is to eat supper. Quibbling and worrying shall not alter circumstances at all."

He then resumed eating, and after a minute we obeyed him and fell to.

As I have said, Wycliffe's translators and most of his poor priests were from among the ranks of the teachers and doctors. It was awkward for me, a mere second-year student, to converse freely with them. They did not expect me to, and it would have been ill-mannered, and—besides all that—it would have done no good for me to make suggestions because nobody would have regarded them. I was too young.

I had come to see Wycliffe at his request, but once our meal was over, I thought it more proper to leave him to his many counselors. So I departed Queen's College. I was nearly to my room when a man stopped me by the door of the hostelry. He seemed familiar, and as soon as he spoke, I recognized him as one from Leicester.

"William Ayleton," he said.

"Yes? What do you want?"

"I am come from your father's farm. The stroke of God has touched him, and he lies awaiting death. You must speak with him by tomorrow morn or never again in this world."

The night was clear and starry, for which I may well have thanked God. Within the hour I was on a horse bound for Leicester, with a dagger in my belt in case of robbers.

At that moment, Wycliffe, papal orders, the arm of the Inquisition, and all that pertained to Oxford, were forgotten. I was but a lad who had not seen his father in a year and a half and would soon never see him again in this world.

Chapter Twenty-one
Oxford Is Left Behind

I came to my father before noon the next day, having stopped in the night when the dark became too deep.

He lay upon his bed with his eyes open, but such labored breaths I had never heard a man draw before. His jaw was clenched tight, as was his right fist. I was afraid when I saw him, but I surprised even myself by striding right to his side and saying quite calmly and tenderly, "Father, your son, William, is here." Then I softly knelt and threw my arm around him.

His eyes turned to look at me, and—after much working of his jaw—he said, "Willie," quite distinctly and gently. I thought he would try to make a joke, as was his habit, to ease me; but the cost of that one word must have warned him to speak directly. So he said, "I'm leaving you, son." And after that he could not speak.

I stayed by him—and when I thought of what a good friend he had been to me, I nearly wept. But I refrained for his sake.

He did not die that day, and so on the next, though he could not speak, I spoke to him. I told him of the translation

I had worked on. I told him of the fighting in London and how we had gotten away. I read to him from his worn and partly ruined old Bible, and I translated much into English, in case his mind could no longer grasp Latin. *"Ego sum resurrectio et vita: qui credit in me, etiamsi mortuus fuerit vivet."* (I am the resurrection and the life: he who believes upon me, although he will have been dead, he shall live.)

He kept his eyes on me as I read or spoke, and I knew he was both grateful for my company and distressed about my future. None had foreseen that his life would be taken so quickly from him, and there had been little preparation. I told him I would keep the farm and become its master. I would take a wife and have children, and I would help John Wycliffe all that I could. This seemed to ease him. I told him nothing of the pope's move against Wycliffe, for I did not want him to be troubled.

Thus, with his mind at ease, he did, on the third day, pass quietly away. His had been a good life, both merry and mournful, and he had lived it like a man through the best and the worst. And I who had been under his rule and who knew him best do testify that he was a good man— as jolly as a minstrel and truer than steel. I laid his bones to rest alongside the grave of my mother and brother.

So I became the master of the farm and my days as a scholar were ended. Yet I kept in touch with Oxford, and knew of it when Wycliffe was moved to Black Hall under a false type of house arrest to placate the pope. And I heard that the Chancellor—for making even that much compromise with the pope—was removed from his seat and another put in his place.

Those papal orders were no false rumors. By January it was well known that orders had been sent to Archbishop Sudbury and Bishop Courtenay as well as to the faculty at Oxford. Presumably, one order had gone to the King.

Wycliffe had been cited to appear at St. Paul's again, but unexpectedly Archbishop Sudbury changed this to his own chapel at Lambeth Palace, across the Thames from

London. The trial was postponed until March, and for that I rejoiced.

Having now some financial means left me by my father, I assembled together those stout men who had been my neighbors all my life. Most of them had heard my father and me talk of Wycliffe, and they were on his side. And they did not like the new pope, Gregory XI, putting his nose into English matters and bringing an Englishman to trial on English soil. It smacked of trying to make the English king a vassal to the pope.

Therefore, come March, a band of a dozen of us set out for Lambeth Palace on horseback. Every man had a dagger or club in his belt, for we were minded, if they put the beloved Doctor to torture or in chains, to rescue him bodily and appeal to the King for a trial. It may seem to have been a bold move to one inexperienced in these matters, but I had heard many stories from the men who had fought in or near Avignon of what a wily fox the pope could be. We had to move faster and strike more quickly, or else the Inquisition would tear Wycliffe away from us, and he would be dead before the King intervened.

Thus it was, on the day of his trial, that we entered Lambeth Palace and pushed aside the porter who would have detained us.

"Think you to get your master's orders before we enter?" thundered one, Wat Fuller. We had left our horses tethered by the roadside for the sake of a fast escape if we needed it. We entered the courtyard on foot.

"Come," one of the others said to the frightened porter. "There shall be no violence done, unless hands are laid on John Wycliffe. Just direct us to the chapel and no blame shall come to you. We are come to keep an eye on things."

The man still hung back, but a gold coin won him over, and he directed us. The chapel at Lambeth was of a good size, with a magnificent altar and many a fine cross set in gold and jewels.

There were some Oxford men inside, seculars as well as monks and friars. Whether they had come to make witness against Wycliffe or to stand by him, I could not tell. Presently, Nicholas Hereford, John Purvey, John Aston, and some of the doctors entered. Purvey greeted me and expressed his sorrow for my father's death.

"It was an unexpected blow," he said. "Yet you should have summoned Wycliffe. It grieved him exceedingly to know that his friend had died."

"How could I?" I asked him. "I knew the Doctor would come, yet his own life hung in the balance. So I left him to prepare his defense for this miserable day."

"I understand. And it is good to see you so well, and—" Here he noticed my companions. He eyed their grim faces and folded arms. "—er, among such doughty companions."

I smiled at him, and he returned to his own comrades, who by this time numbered as many as we. Some knew me and gave me greeting, but several—including Hereford— looked alarmed at seeing such a band of men. For the sake of surprise we had covered our weapons, but any man with a brain in his head might have guessed why a band of yeoman farmers would appear at a trial of a professor of theology. It was certainly not to learn Latin, nor to weigh out the complicated disputations which would take place. When yeoman farmers came in a group, they came to *do* something.

At last we heard the ringing of a bell, and we made way for the procession of examiners. Across the way, John Purvey looked me in the eye, and I sensed he was glad we had come.

Chapter Twenty-two
An Unexpected End

John Wycliffe entered a short time after the examiners were seated. We gave him the same respect in making way for him as we had done for the prelates. And indeed, Wycliffe in his faded brown robe and bare feet drew more reverence from us than Sudbury in all his linen and jewels.

"Shame!" one of my band called out to the Archbishop.

Bishop William Courtenay thundered from his throne-like chair, "Silence! Silence in the House of God!" He stood up. "There shall be no disruption here, for this is the House of God!"

"Domus mea domus orationis est!" John Aston, among the Oxford men, cried out.

Courtenay, about to sit down, rose again, and two men-at-arms entered, but Aston subsided.

"What did he say?" Wat Fuller whispered to me.

" *'My house is a house of prayer,'* " I told him and added the rest, " *'But you have made it a den of thieves.'* It is something the Lord said to the Hebrew prelates in his day. That doctor over there was challenging the Bishop with it."

Wat gave a low guffaw. "That stung His Grace, all right."

"Would to God we could whip them out of here as the Lord did in His day," I said in a low voice.

Courtenay at last took his seat, and the soldiers who had come in retired.

"John of Wycliffe, you are accused on eighteen points of heresy," Sudbury said. "I shall read them for this court."

The trial, of course, was in Latin, and my followers were impatient with the drawn out pomp and ceremony that these rogues insisted upon. There were several Dominicans of the Inquisition seated among the prelates, and my fingers itched for my dagger. For it would have been service to my King and to England to see to it that they never left Lambeth alive. Yet this was now the England of Richard, not Edward, and it was Richard who would have to give the word.

All the same, after Sudbury's lengthy recitation was over, I motioned to my fellows to be ready. At any moment Wycliffe might be committed to the dungeons to be questioned, and that would mean hot irons and the rack.

It seemed as though they were minded to let Wycliffe speak, but just as he began, we all heard a tremendous jingling of men in mail shirts.

We made way for a man, dressed in velvets of black and purple, with a sword at his side, and his gray head bare of any hat. He was accompanied by four or five of his men, also armed. I did not know the sign of their livery, but this man was obviously a knight by his bearing and clothes, and his handsome face was crossed here and there with scars, so that one could see he had been to the wars.

Wycliffe stopped, and all eyes went to this hale old knight, who stood straight and tall as any young man.

"I, Sir Lewis Clifford, knight of the Garter and servant of his Majesty, King Richard II, do humbly beg the pardon of you all," he announced, speaking in English. "I am sent as emissary of Joan of Kent, mother of the King, to this court to inform them touching our beloved servant, John of Wycliffe, who has rendered faithful service to the Crown and to England. Whereas the said John Wycliffe has been tried and found innocent of all heresies before the faculty of Oxford University, and whereas the same Reverend Doctor has assisted us much in the past, and whereas the same Doctor is aged and infirm and worthy of reverence and dignity, we hereby do confirm that the civil law shall not touch this said John Wycliffe. This Church court may and shall proceed and may pass judgment, but the civil law finds no condemnation in this man, nor any act on his part to necessitate torture or imprisonment." The worthy knight paused as we raised a loud cheer for his message.

The faces of the prelates had gone from their stern dignity to white-faced shock. In effect, Joan of Kent had forbidden any man to lay a hand on Wycliffe, regardless of the verdict of the Church court.

Sir Lewis Clifford continued, "I, being the emissary of Joan of Kent, shall maintain my presence here to make sure that her wishes are carried out."

I know not whether the knight had arranged it this way, but just then there burst into the room a band of men led by John of Northampton, sheriff of London and a man friendly and generous to our cause. At sight of Sir Lewis Clifford, his band raised a loud cheer, and we joined in.

The trial proceeded, but on a very different footing. When Wycliffe spoke, all were silent, but as soon as one of the prelates spoke, all the Londoners would burst out with catcalls, whistles, applause, and other noise. The prelates—even Bishop Courtenay—could do nothing, not with Lewis Clifford there.

At last the bishops passed their sentence. They forbade Wycliffe from preaching any of the eighteen points in his sermons or teaching them at Oxford.

It was a sentence that Wycliffe ignored. Thronged with his friends, amid many congratulations, he was carried from the hall in safety and peace.

Chapter Twenty-three
The Sufferings of John Wycliffe
December, 1427

I have purposely ended my narration at our triumph in Lambeth chapel. Indeed, it was the last time that I ever saw Hereford or Repton or most of the others.

Not long after Wycliffe's trial, he was questioning the Church's doctrine of transubstantiation, the belief that the bread and wine in the mass are transformed into the very body and blood of Jesus our Lord.

Wycliffe, schooled as he was in Scripture, could no longer accept this doctrine, and he searched for the true answer. He was, as he had once remarked to me, a man in a very dark cave, knowing where the pitfalls lay but not sure of the way. He had none to assist him in his understanding, no man as well schooled as he was to point out his errors in thinking.

But when he said that the doctrine of the Eucharist was blasphemy, there were many who turned against him. The Duke of Lancaster, for one, tried to persuade him to let it remain a mystery. And when the Doctor would not, the Duke let him be.

Oxford expelled him. Yes, Oxford, the place that he had helped to make great. He had to leave, and so he retired to his parish at Lutterworth, where I visited him several times. Though leaving Oxford pained him, he was not at a loss. He immediately began writing treatises on the errors in the Church and sermon outlines for priests who were seeking the truth. Visitors poured in to see him. Many an impoverished parish priest came knocking on his door to seek help and guidance, and Wycliffe never turned any away.

His people loved him, and he was careful of their needs, both material and spiritual. He freely gave to the poor of his parish, and in times of sickness he could—as long as his health stayed by him—still be found helping the sick, even as he had done years ago on the streets of Oxford.

Bishop Courtenay could not touch Wycliffe, but he attacked all those at Oxford of Wycliffe's persuasions. The "poor priests" were named *Lollards* in derision, some saying they talked ceaselessly, "La-la-la-la—"

Purvey, Aston, and Repton, as well as many I did not know, were brought to trial. A few Lollards were imprisoned, even burned, when they refused to give up their beliefs or publicly disavow them. But most of them recanted. Nicholas Hereford fled to Rome to appeal to the pope, and he was imprisoned. Having recanted, Purvey and Aston became parish priests. Repton recanted and stayed at Oxford.

The Doctor did not live much longer. I would often visit him, and he was always warm to me. Nor did he ever condemn those who had deserted him.

He, with his keen foresight, had known that troubles would plague him. He met them bravely and continued to write against the abuses in the Church. I was able to help him a little.

There came the days of the Great Schism, when there was a pope in Rome and another in Avignon, and both were hiring armies to slaughter the followers of the other. Helpless peasants were massacred like sheep in those days. Well did Wycliffe conclude that the pope was not a leader of the Church but the Antichrist—one who came claiming to stand in the person of Christ on earth while amassing money and power, defending error, and killing the innocent, all to preserve himself.

His proclamation that the pope was the Antichrist was his last great message. He wrote on it and boldly preached it and taught it to many of the yeomen who came to listen to him. The wrath of the Church waxed hotter, but it could not touch him.

Wycliffe died quietly, of a stroke. And many did mourn him. The fires of persecution waxed hotter, and I wondered— with a wife and children of my own—what I should do if I were summoned. But I never was, I suppose because I was not a priest.

John Aston returned to the truth, for which I thank God, and began again to preach the Holy Scriptures. They hunted him, but he escaped into hiding. And many a time did he sit at my table.

John Purvey also returned to the truth and made his escape from Courtenay's hounds. His health was broken—I think from the inward grief he'd suffered over deserting Wycliffe and the truth. When he came to my door, I took him in and served him as best I could. Nonetheless he died, a man aged before his time. I feared that his bones would be burned, and so I quietly buried him alongside my father, as though he were my own brother. May God have mercy on John Purvey, who—though he fell—translated most of the Scripture from Latin into English. And I do testify that God raised him up again from the pit where he fell; so I trust God will raise him up on the last day, and his grief be forgotten.

Nicholas Hereford, I judge, perhaps lost his mind while in prison. He escaped from Rome and got back to England, where he recanted most vehemently, once Courtenay got hold of him. And then he began to persecute the Lollards and preach against them. It was he who had betrayed Aston and Purvey to the Inquisition. It all passed belief for treachery. And Hereford, though I often privately thought him foolish, had never seemed a traitor to me. It seemed more likely that his tormentors had driven him out of his mind. The last I ever heard of him was that he had joined a strict monastery, but that was years ago. May God also pity Nicholas Hereford.

I at this writing am an old man, only three years short of my threescore and ten. And they tell me that Wycliffe's bones have been dug up and burned and cast into the river that leads to the sea. The Church—she thinks—has had her revenge.

But, as I hear it, Wycliffe's writings had already touched one man in Bohemia, John Huss, whom the Church burned several years ago. And though both Wycliffe and Huss be dead, there are rumors of unrest in that small country, unrest caused by those who seek true religion.

In England, King Henry rules hand in glove with the pope, but not forever, I think.

We are still here—the Lollards, I mean. Did you guess it? Yes, I have become a "poor priest." And I will tell you this: the writings of Wycliffe have been driven out of Oxford, but they can be found in every other nook in England. Indeed, many a time I have talked with an Oxford scholar on the road and have seen God open his heart to the truth.

This is what St. Paul meant when he spoke of Christians as being pressed but never pinned. The Church rages, but the truth goes on. Many a stout English yeoman embraces it in these days and leads his family in true godly worship.

John Wycliffe was our morning star. When all was darkest and England lay asleep in the deadly arms of the papacy, God sent him to us. The Scripture has come to England. What will hold it back? Soon—though perhaps not in my lifetime—the dawn will break, and there will be a new day in England.

Author's Note

John Wycliffe has been called the Morning Star of the Reformation, and it is true that Luther, Calvin, Colet, and Bilney were influenced by his works while they were studying their way out of the maze of Roman Catholic error. He was, as I said in this book, a man very much alone in his pursuit of truth, for in that day men were governed by the Church at Rome, and Scripture was a closed book to the common man. Wycliffe's proclamation that Scripture alone is the rule of the Christian faith came directly from the Holy Spirit's leading as he studied the Scripture in his early days of Oxford. Wycliffe's dream of making it possible for poor rough peasants to recite Bible verses and to understand the great doctrines taught in Scripture was considered outlandish. The idea of putting anything holy in the hands of coarse peasants was thought vulgar and sacrilegious.

Sudbury, Courtenay, the Duke of Lancaster, and the poor priests mentioned in this book are all drawn from history. Although it was Wycliffe's idea to translate the Latin Vulgate Bible into English, most of the actual translation was probably done by John Purvey, with considerable help from Nicholas

Hereford. John Aston, a mathematical genius who is still acknowledged for some of his treatises written while at Oxford, also helped them and went preaching in the countryside. Sadly, all three of them did recant their beliefs under the fear of torture or death. But Purvey and Aston relapsed; that is, they returned to their former "heresies." In effect, they returned to the truth of God's Word in opposition to the Roman Catholic Church. Aston went into hiding and preached where he could. Purvey, as far as historical records show, disappeared and was never heard from again. Some people assume that he died shortly after he began again to follow the teaching of Scripture.

Sebastian and William Ayleton, Fleet Nigel, and Giles are all fictional characters, though they were created to represent types common enough in England at that time. William represents what the Lollards became. Wycliffe's beliefs—within about one generation of his death—moved from the scholarly halls of Oxford into the humbler halls of the yeoman's abode. It became an underground movement that grew with the growing middle class. Throughout the hottest persecutions that were to come until the sixteenth century, neither king nor pope could stamp out the Lollards. Ultimately, they fused with the Protestant Reformation or were absorbed into other movements.

The riots that I have recorded, as well as the Pestilence (the Black Death), really did occur. Most of the events that pertained to Wycliffe are taken from history, including the shouting match between John of Gaunt and Bishop Courtenay in the Chapel of the Blessed Virgin at St. Paul's Cathedral. I hope that this book has succeeded in making the fourteenth century come alive for the reader. But mostly, I hope that it shows what can happen when the Bible is put into the hands of a man—scholar or farmer—and he gives himself to studying it seriously.